advice for fighting for change will serve as a modern moral compass for anyone willing to get to work. We are the superheroes we've been waiting for, and John gives us very specific directions on how to fashion our capes, tie them tightly, and then take flight."

—Shannon Watts, founder of Moms Demand Action

"In his new book, *Hope and Other Superpowers*, Pavlovitz reminds us that in a world that seems dangerous and confusing, all the answers exist in our own humanity. Small acts of compassion and kindness are powerful. The author shares a plan for living a life of activism through one's own humanity. The idea is to not be intimidated by the cruelty around us, but to live boldly and to expose the world's beauty through our actions and words. Ultimately, in order to regain a sense of good in this country, a sense of community and concern for all, it's up to us. While that may seem like a daunting task, it's really not. Pavlovitz simplifies the path in this book and reminds us how powerful humanity can be."

—Steve Kerr, head coach, Golden State Warriors

HOPE

AND OTHER SUPERPOWERS

*A Life-Affirming, Love-Defending,
Butt-Kicking, World-Saving Manifesto*

JOHN PAVLOVITZ

SIMON & SCHUSTER

NEW YORK   LONDON   TORONTO   SYDNEY   NEW DELHI

Simon & Schuster
1230 Avenue of the Americas
New York, NY 10020

First Simon & Schuster hardcover edition November 2018

SIMON & SCHUSTER and colophon are registered trademarks of Simon & Schuster, Inc.

For information about special discounts for bulk purchases,
please contact Simon & Schuster Special Sales
at 1-866-506-1949 or business@simonandschuster.com.

The Simon & Schuster Speakers Bureau can bring authors to your live event.
For more information, or to book an event contact the Simon & Schuster Speakers Bureau
at 1-866-248-3049 or visit our website at www.simonspeakers.com.

Interior design by Ruth Lee-Mui

Manufactured in the United States of America

10   9   8   7   6   5   4   3   2   1

Library of Congress Cataloging-in-Publication Data
Names: Pavlovitz, John, author.
Title: Hope and other superpowers : a life affirming, love-defending,
    butt-kicking, world-saving manifesto / John Pavlovitz.
Description: New York : Simon & Schuster, 2018.
Identifiers: LCCN 2018015318I ISBN 9781501179655 (hardcover) I
    ISBN 9781501179679 (trade paper) I ISBN 9781501179662 (e-book)
Subjects: LCSH: Heroism. I Hope. I Caring. I Humanitarianism. I Social action.
Classification: LCC BJ1533.H47 P38 2018 I DDC 170/.44—dc23
LC record available at https://lccn.loc.gov/2018015318

ISBN 978-1-5011-7965-5
ISBN 978-1-5011-7966-2 (ebook)

This book is dedicated with great affection to my mother, Ginny Pavlovitz.

Since before I was born, you've given me a front row seat to a heroic life.

I love you and I love being your son.

And to the LGBTQ community, for waking up every day,

bravely walking out into the world, and being superheroes.

CONTENTS

CONTENTS

PART THREE: TRAINING GROUND 179

NEWS FROM METROPOLIS

I can remember when I first figured out that I wasn't a superhero. I was around six years old, running through the woods behind our house, when I came upon an imposing section of rusted barbed wire in my path. It might have been a formidable obstacle for any *mortal* child, but certainly, I'd concluded, not for me. Weaned on a healthy diet of comic books and Saturday morning cartoons, I was fully confident that my latent supernatural abilities were ready to spring forth and my impending mythical career fighting injustice and tyranny was about to begin in dramatically soundtracked fashion. Without blinking, I doubled my resolve and sprinted harder toward the fence, fueled by the excitement that this would be my grand origin story, the moment the planet would be forever altered by the birth of a legend. With only a few feet to go before I collided with the twisted strands of metal, I launched myself from the ground, anticipating that I would soon be transcending not only the fence but the surrounding treetops as well on my way to glory. I came about a fence and some treetops short. Four decades later the large scar on my left calf is a permanent, tangible reminder of the day when I proved to be just a little bit less than super. I imagine you, too, carry both the visible (and hidden) scars of the times you tried to fly and instead came crashing hard down to earth, days you faced your mortality and skinned your knee.

The desire for significance is buried deep within all of us. We all hope to leave a lasting mark on this place in the brief sliver of time we're here, to have lives fueled by purpose and filled with joy—to craft legacies that long outlive us. We all want to do something decidedly *super*, and most of us begin our journeys believing that we can, fully expecting to be extraordinary. But somewhere along the way, we find ourselves weakened by the pain and disappointment in our path, by our perceived shortcomings and missteps, by cruel words we receive, and by the disheartening circumstances in which we find ourselves. Or maybe we begin to dwell on the swirling, ever-present storm of bad news, until we're gradually overtaken by a growing sense of helplessness in the face of it all. Little by little, sometimes almost undetectably, all these internal doubts and exterior obstacles prevent us from aspiring to the rarefied air we once believed our destiny. Instead, we resign ourselves to the muddy ruts of the ordinary, deciding that this is good enough, that we shouldn't bother reaching for more, or doing more, or believing that any kind of *more* is actually even possible. And yet, at no point in recent memory have these kinds of apathy and cynicism been more dangerous, because the world you and I are standing on is in desperate need of people still willing to *reach* and *do* and *believe* and, most of all, to be fierce caretakers of hope.

For each of us there are precise pivot points in this life, turbulent times when we're called upon to face something that feels bigger than we can handle or to carry more than we believe we can bear. The 2016 presidential election was such a moment for me and millions of others. It was an existential earthquake, a seismic upheaval in the bedrock of our *normal* that rattled our foundations and is still sending us regular emotional aftershocks. Looking back I'd felt the tremors coming from a long way off. Over the course of the campaign, my blog, *Stuff That Needs To Be Said*, had grown almost exponentially. I'd been slowly but steadily building a global audience, but as the campaign wound on and as I began speaking more explicitly into the intersection of faith and politics in America, tens of thousands of new people started connecting and joining the conversation each month. It was a wildly diverse group assembling around the hub of my words, people of every religious tradition, political affiliation, and personal worldview. And yet, there was a singular thread of affinity holding us all together: the desire for a hope that could not be shaken—and it was about to be greatly shaken.

Having lived half of my life as a minister and caregiver, I've had a front row seat to people who were hurting, and been given sacred access to their deepest grief and their most tender wounds. I've served as a local church pastor for twenty years, spending the last four also overseeing a large global online community, and even though I've grown somewhat accustomed to strangers baring their souls to me, over the last year or two it feels as if the pain and despair have escalated. People feel like the world is upside down, and they are reeling from the disorientation. A friend of mine captured the frustration succinctly as we shared a coffee a few weeks after the 2016 election. Through tears she asked: "Doesn't anyone remember how to be a decent human being, for Christ's sake?" I reminded her that yes, lots of people do. People of every religious tradition, political affiliation, and nation of origin instinctively know there is a better way to live, and they want to figure out how to unearth it. They want to live valiantly and bravely, to be the antidote to the despair that has so afflicted us. They want to help us reconnect with our best selves—and with one another. I bet you're one of these people. I bet you feel that same *holy discontent* the great storytellers have spoken about for millennia, that heavy burden on a human heart that compels someone to seek a deeper kind of living, a better way of being here, a more intentional ordinary. I think you share that same gravitational pull toward goodness that compels heroes to run headlong into the maelstrom to save people when others scatter. I believe you, too, want to live heroically. These urgent yearnings are the reason this book was born: because these days *are* unprecedented, because there *is* so much at stake, and because complacency and inaction now are more dangerous than ever.

Many of us are lamenting the despair and divisiveness around us, aching for something more redemptive but no longer sure how to get to it from where we stand. We've watched helplessly as people have grown emboldened in the kind of bigotry they'd once kept concealed. We've witnessed unabashed hatred regularly trending nationally. We've seen new fractures develop or old wounds reopen in our families, marriages, and friendships. Public discourse has dissolved, and a baseline of decency that we've always counted on has evaporated. We're all desperately straining for something to sustain us—something to right all that feels so wrong around us and to calm everything that feels unsettled within us. We are looking for connectedness at a time when disconnection is epidemic.

Most of us have made the mistake of looking for such hope outside ourselves—a writer, a politician, a preacher, a musician, a celebrity. But friends, the truth is that *we* are the heroes we've been waiting for. It isn't the sky that holds our hope for the planet, it's the mirror, and the time has come for us to reconnect to the sacred, essential *why* of our lives and to live more fully from that place. We need to rediscover the optimism of our youth, to remember when the desire to change the world felt reasonable and not shamefully naive, when doing something heroic seemed possible and didn't merit ridicule or a rolling of the eyes. In times when people seem increasingly immune to others' pain, we need to unapologetically wield hearts still willing to bleed, and then affix them to our sleeves and step into the daylight looking for gaps in the world that we alone can fill.

The vital question at the heart of these pages is, "What kind of person does the world need right now?" The way you and I answer that question together will craft our precise job descriptions, the specific heroes we are each called to be here and now in this far-too-short section of the bigger story that we get to share. This is what the superheroes we all love do: they see the dangers and injustices in the world, and they run into those terrifying voids believing they can save the day or that they will die trying.

And this heroic existence we're called to is about doing the small and simple things that most people lose sight of, the things that may not make the news or trend on social media, but that generate beautiful ripples nonetheless. It's about chipping away at the image of the life we think we're supposed to have and uncovering the life that we deserve to live, the kind the planet is made better by. It's about understanding that we have far more power at our disposal than we're aware of. There is a transcendent way of living that can begin to alter the planet in real time—right now—and it's fully accessible to each of us regardless of what we do, where we live, or how much influence we *think* we have. That's the amazing truth at work here: the world has always been transformed by fully ordinary people whose willingness to show up, to brave damage, and to risk failure yielded extraordinary results.

Perhaps this mission feels daunting and quite a bit beyond reach right now, but we'll get there together. As we walk through these pages, my hope is that monumental challenges will begin to shrink down to manageable goals, and rather than feeling frustration, you will find a new clarity of vision, fueled by the realization that you are uniquely qualified and positioned to make a substantive difference in this world. In days like these, when apathy and denial are so tempting, the very first step is simply giving a damn. (And the good news is, you already do, otherwise you wouldn't be reading this book). With this glorious damn-giving we begin to write a new story for ourselves and for the world.

We know that stories are transformative, whether they're

stretched out across massive screens, printed onto pages, or played out in front of us in flesh and blood through people we see and know and love. This is why we treasure these stories and why we wait in line to see them. In other people's experiences we find affinity, inspiration, and the invitation to be a better version of ourselves. They often become the catalyst for our own metamorphosis. During our journey within these pages, we'll step into the stories of other ordinary superhumans and allow the way they triumph against adversity, despair, and opposition to launch *us* into the stratosphere of *our* greater purpose. These examples of simple acts of perseverance and personal activism will lead you into your calling in ways that may not (and don't need to) look anything like theirs.

In this adventure we'll identify ways of cultivating key traits (ordinary superpowers) that will improve our lives and bolster our humanity, and we'll identify our unique gifts and weapons in the quest to become heroic. We'll think about the weaknesses (our personal Kryptonite) that leave us all vulnerable and prepare for the adversaries and villains we'll surely face along the way. We'll look back on our personal journeys and remember how they have been punctuated with beauty and wonder, and we'll see how our story has specifically prepared us and can propel us forward.

And in the same way that superheroes don't just work alone but in teams of other extraordinary people, we'll learn to leverage the exponential power of community by connecting with like-hearted humans, with the ultimate goal of creating a global movement of radical goodness.

Hope and Other Superpowers isn't a self-help book—it's a life-affirming, love-defending, butt-kicking manifesto, a rallying cry for an unwaveringly joyful revolution that we get to set into motion. It is a personalized guide to being a better human being, creating a more meaningful life, and building a better planet in the process. It is a summoning of our alter egos, a crystallizing of our inner convictions, and an amplifying of our voices—empowering us to work together for as long as it takes for the world that *should be* to become the world that *is*.

In 1871, while preaching a sermon opposing slavery in America, Unitarian minister Theodore Parker said, "The arc of the universe bends toward justice." His words were echoed almost a century later by Dr. Martin Luther King, Jr., as solace for those looking around at the unbridled bigotry of the day and feeling like the decent people were losing. Embedded in this phrase is the promise that over time, in ways that we can't always perceive from where we're standing at a given moment, humanity *does* evolve toward goodness. This idea can be useful in preventing us from being overwhelmed by the circumstances of the day. It can give us the necessary perspective of seeing life from thirty thousand feet, as opposed to the furiously shaking ground we stand upon—like stepping back from a van Gogh painting to make wonderful sense of what up close appears to be a muddled, disorienting mess. We who reside in *this* here and now need to understand that though the arc of the universe does bend, it does not bend without us and our efforts and strength. Humanity is the irresistible force shaping the crescent, with every single life and every infinitesimal, seemingly unimportant decision adjusting its path in ways we can't measure or imagine. With each movement, with every action, the curvature changes ever so slightly. It is changing in the seconds it takes me to type these words, and you to read them. Every single moment is a movement, one way or the other. This means that *we* are the arc benders. We are the people the world needs; not passive victims of these difficult times, but powerful participants in them. We are mighty coauthors of the story we now find ourselves in, and together we can help write something redemptive that can twist the plot. We each come heavily armed to this endeavor. Our abilities, talents, and passions are all forces we bring to bear on that arc—and so we live intentionally, realizing how pregnant with possibility every second is. There are no inconsequential choices, no ordinary moments, no meaningless days. We are daily waging a war to be present and alive and engaged. As in the pages of a comic book, the bad guys are relentless, and so we have to be equally steadfast in our convictions now. We need to serve as the guardians and stewards of hope, and remind the world that no matter how noisily hatred bellows through a bullhorn, love will always have the last, loudest word.

Friend, if you've been waiting for the right moment to step from the shadows and into the fray—this would be the one. Consider this book your personal, urgent invitation, like a spotlight signal cutting through the night sky, calling you to don your cape and cowl and to move toward the need outside your door. Metropolis is in peril, and you are within earshot of its citizens' frantic pleas for someone to give a damn and do something. Grab a mirror, true believer; you might see a superhero staring at you. It's time to suit up, take a deep breath, and get ready to fly.

PART ONE

THE HERO IN ALL OF US

WHO DO YOU THINK YOU ARE? The question is often asked of superheroes in times of confrontation, by an enraged supervillain trying to get inside their heads and derail them. It is a targeted attack on the protagonists' capabilities, their motives, their very identity. You and I receive similar interrogation from those who oppose us, as they attempt to dismiss our perspective or destroy our confidence. Our adversaries challenge us to justify ourselves or defend our actions or prove our worth. But asked of ourselves, this question can be an invitation, one that helps us see how our specific gifts and particular experiences have uniquely prepared us to do planet-changing, hope-giving work. Who do *you* think you are? Consider your answer carefully. It can save the world.

ONE

ORIGIN STORIES

Who wouldn't want to be Peter Parker? Sure, being bitten by a radioactive spider had to hurt like hell initially, but you have to admit the resulting upside was pretty sweet: the ability to climb walls, sense incoming danger, shoot webs from his wrists, and catapult himself across rooftops during rush hour—what's not to love about that? For most of us, our teenage years were a prolonged, stumbling, hormone-addled mess, so a brief moment of subatomic agony would have been well worth the benefits it afforded in expediency alone. If you're going to go through the dizzying arrival of puberty anyway, at least the transformation could be quick, dramatic, and awe-inspiring. Peter was one of the lucky ones. His metamorphosis happened in one brilliant, cataclysmic instant—instead of over a few brutal years of awkwardness, heart-break, and bad skin. Unlike most of us, he received the payoff in a matter of breathtaking seconds. He didn't have to wait to become amazing or hope he'd one day be super. Meanwhile, if you're anything like me, you probably feel like you're still patiently waiting and hoping for heroic things to happen in you.

That's why we all love to see superheroes being born in pages or on-screen. There's something magical about those beginnings that moves us. Whether they're bitten by a radioactive spider, injected with a secret government superserum, implanted with a steel skeleton, or overexposed to hulkifying gamma rays, every great hero has an amazing origin story, a precise moment when he or she is called upon by circumstance, fate, or providence to do something extraordinary, something meaningful, something altogether history-shifting. It's thrilling to watch human beings mutating from nondescript, regular schlubs like you and me into the monumental stuff of legend, to see them struggle to comprehend the gravity of the moment, to recognize the responsibility of access to such great power—and ultimately to run, swing, or fly headlong into their destiny. Over and over again we line up to breathe in these mythologies, because we love the idea of being thrust into stratospheric glory instead of being stuck here on the ground with the rest of the mere mortals and gawking bystanders. We inhabit daily lives that tend to feel decidedly *nonsuper,* a repetitive cycle of mundane tasks and soul-draining busywork made of laundry loads, traffic jams, and dental appointments, and as we get older it becomes a lot easier to hope vicariously through someone else's story than our own. We gradually lose our ability to dream.

Children don't usually struggle with such effortless imagination and boundless optimism. My eight-year-old daughter, Selah, certainly doesn't. I'd call her primary superpower *explosiveness.* She ricochets through this life full speed and wide open, bouncing through her days fueled by a combustible cocktail of joy, confidence, expectancy, and Skittles. She fully believes that she's unstoppable, and she's not alone. *Most* children are peerless superheroes—just ask them. Sit down with a group of second graders and wonder out loud, "Who here is a dancer?" and every hand will go up. Ask, "Are there any artists in the room?" Each will volunteer with unabashed enthusiasm. Interrogate them further: "How many of you are *super-smart?*" To a child, they will gladly cop to their brilliance without a trace of arrogance, seemingly fully aware of their infinite capacity to do beautiful things and blissfully ignorant of any weaknesses. Ask the same question of a group of teenagers or adults, and you will get a decidedly different response: an array of caveats and qualifiers and self-critical comments. You'll see people avoiding eye contact and internally disqualifying themselves. That's because over time, we experience enough failure and rejection, we hear enough about our flaws and deficiencies, until we finally concede that *this* is our true identity, that whatever we are now is the best we can hope for. We begin to hear in our heads the voices of our critics and adversaries, of deceased parents, ex-spouses, and former bosses, and we ratify the gaslighter's lie that we are far less than spectacular. This is why embracing your inherent and abiding *superness* isn't about figuring out how to *become* anything but about realizing what you've forgotten about yourself since you were young, the truth you've lost along the way about who you are, what you're made of, and your capacity to be great. Like my daughter, you, too, were designed to live wide open and to dance and sing and dream wildly. You simply need to remember the ass-kicking glory you were made for and to prepare yourself for the ever-present opportunities you have to still be super.

Every hero is pulled into significance differently. Batman rises from the ashes of his parents' murder to defend a crime-riddled Gotham. Wonder Woman feels compelled to come to the aid of outnumbered Allied soldiers facing the Third Reich, after being cared for by one of them. Black Panther fully claims his birthright as king after realizing his nation's former missteps. Spider-Man is transformed after recognizing the great responsibility accompanying his great power. Black Widow is moved to make amends for her deadly assassin's past. They *all* become undeniably heroic, yet in ways and circumstances that look nothing alike and with completely unique motivations. In the same way, you and I will each receive a one of a kind, time-sensitive invitation to step into a better version of ourselves: a personal tragedy, a national crisis, a cause that moves us, or a desire to use a gift for the good of others. This is the beauty of our origin stories: they are completely personalized. They are unprecedented occasions. We become specifically heroic as we move to answer a call that we alone can answer—because we are the only ones able to hear it.

On November 9, 2016, one of my calls came quite literally overnight. I'd spent the early morning hours following the presidential election fielding messages that began pouring in from all sorts of people in acute crisis, men and women seeing what felt like their most terrifying nightmares springing to life. As quickly as I could reply to one, dozens more came in. The scale and velocity of the pain were overwhelming—and continue to be. Later that morning, while it was still dark, without having slept more than a few scattered moments, I sat down and composed a blog post called "Here's Why We Grieve Today," hoping to synthesize the heaviness people had been sharing with me, the sense of loss and missed opportunity so many were feeling and trying to process. By the end of the day, two and a half million people had read the post—and by Friday of that week nearly four million. I began to realize that this was an opportunity to help people from a distance. I could walk with them as they grieved by giving voice to their confusion, fear, and anguish. I could put words to people's pain, I could loudly advocate for those who were being marginalized, and I could openly resist a corrupt power that was gaining traction. Even in the sadness that I and so many others felt in those hours, I found solace in realizing that my years as a pastor and activist and writer and social media presence had all left me uniquely positioned and prepared to help people in that precise moment. My platform and my words could be weapons used to push back against the terrors—and I was grateful to be drafted into battle.

I wasn't alone in the fight either. After the 2016 election, millions of Americans responded to what was their worst-case scenario by allowing it to catalyze them into a level of activism and engagement they'd never imagined themselves capable of. A generation of ordinary superheroes was born, as people used whatever they had at their disposal to defend the country they loved and the issues that burdened them. But we see similar opportunities for metamorphosis much closer to home—the loss of loved ones or career changes or unexpected illness or needs in our community. Adversity (ours or others') is always an invitation to be transformed, and like it or not we can find plenty of that the longer we're here. The suffering we see in the world, the divisions in our nation, the disappointments we accrue, and the struggles of parenting, marriage, and career are all potential places where either our defeat can be finalized—or our destiny clarified. They can be sources of growing bitterness or spaces for cultivating hope. The difference between the two is often a matter of the lenses we view these moments with, and the small choices we make in a million seemingly unremarkable moments.

Though we'd probably prefer it, we rarely discover the heroic mettle within us until we reach what we believe to be the limits of our ability and tolerance for pain. And that is one of the difficult ironies of this life: tragedy is an opportunity to become something we couldn't become in any other way. The Christian tradition calls this "rejoicing in trials": the awareness in the moment that present difficulty is infinitely valuable and uniquely formative. In layman's terms, it just means to be glad when you're getting the shit kicked out of you because that shit-kicking is rebuilding you in beautiful ways despite the bruises and gashes you sustain. Whenever Fantastic Four team member (and talking pile of orange rocks) the Thing has endured enough pummeling from his adversaries and is ready to turn the tables, he shouts his famous rallying cry: "It's clobberin' time!" and proceeds to lay waste to the bad guys. Yet that victorious, redemptive moment never comes until he has been sufficiently throttled himself.

For me, life came clobberin' four years ago, when my father died very suddenly while on a vacation cruise. When I got the call from my younger brother with the news of his passing, I dropped to the ground in front of our house and felt the world cave in around me. As my tears fell onto the grass beneath me, I was as helpless and broken as I'd ever been, a full-blown Armageddon exploding inside my head. Later that week, I sat across from my dear friend Brenda in a crowded coffee shop. Encouragement is Brenda's greatest superpower, among many. Through the thick haze of my grief, I remember her looking into my tear-blurred, bloodshot eyes and saying, "John, this is going to give you a layer of compassion that you've never had. You'll understand people's pain in a deeper way than ever before, and you'll be able to help them." It wasn't much consolation then, but she was right, because that's how grief and sorrow and all varieties of emotional catastrophe work: you never really *get it* until you're grieving or hurting or struggling. There's no way to comprehend real loss other than to walk through it—and once you have, you want to walk with others because you understand how terribly exhausting it is to endure alone.

Just a few days after losing my father I started writing about my grief on my blog. I did it primarily to try to retain my sanity, but soon realized that it was encouraging other people who were also in the thick blackness of what I began to refer to as the Grief Valley. Their solidarity from a distance, in turn, helped lift me through those days, and it gave me some measure of solace to know that something productive was coming out of my profound pain. I ended up documenting that first year on the blog and have continued recording the things I've learned along the way about the attrition of loss. I've since led retreats on grief, counseled hundreds of people, and reached millions of others through writing—all by doing nothing more than telling my story and showing my scars.

Brenda knew what she was talking about. She knew the

productive nature of suffering and that time and distance would help me—as it will surely help you—figure out how to channel defeats and deaths into something life-affirming. And that's a key lesson to embrace as you try to be the kind of person the world needs, the kind who can save the world; the adversity you've endured and the battles you've weathered, as terrible as they are in real time, are necessary to call you to a deeper place of compassion and kindness than you would otherwise be capable of.

Ironically, similar moments of total desperation are an absolute blast to read in a book or see on the big screen. We love it when our caped crusaders are pushed to the very brink of obliteration, to the very last thread of their final rope, because *that* makes their coming victory all the more thrilling. We see all that they've endured, and it makes us root for them even harder, and the celebration in the closing minutes becomes all the more jubilant. But in real life, we never see these times as climactic narrative pivot points or necessary character-defining moments set to music. We rarely find ourselves in the middle of everything hitting the fan and think, "This is going to make an awesome story! This is going to help people one day!" We almost never experience pain and imagine what it is producing in us other than discomfort, and we certainly don't welcome it like a dear friend arriving on our doorstep, or see it as an incubator for our best selves.

And that may be the initial switch that needs to take place in us as we embrace our superhumanness during days that feel oppressively heavy. Maybe we need to take some time to purposefully rewind and chart the past moments of our lives—recording every crushing defeat, every failed venture, every aha moment, every broken relationship, every wonderful surprise—and to take stock of how these experiences have uniquely prepared and strengthened us. Not only that, but we can see in the rearview mirror how we've cultivated values and honed skills and acquired resources in the process. We can be encouraged that yes, we are qualified, because we've paid our dues over time and in tears and through trials. My friend Ed calls this a crossroads map, the retrospective look at all we've endured so that we can spot and acknowledge what it's done within us. If we can see the redemptive value of all the horrible things we've walked through to this second, maybe it can help us the next time we face a trial or feel forsaken. Rather than simply going through something painful or witnessing tragedy and falling apart, we can pause to consider how it might be shaping us. We can be aware that we *are* being forged in the fire of present struggle. We can begin transforming our disappointments and frustrations into calling even as we grieve them. It means we can see others' burdens and move to alleviate them. It means we can unapologetically give voice to concealed dreams we've been carrying around in silence. It means we can walk boldly into the day believing we have something to give the world that it needs and that no one else is capable of giving. It means we can be heroic in more than just our daydreams but in our real nightmares, too.

When I was a kid in a suburban small town in central New York, my father owned a shoe store, which was sandwiched between a dry cleaner and a dance studio. The pungent smell of the pant presses from the former and the staccato rhythms on the hardwood floor from the latter are both deeply embedded in me as sense memories. Behind the old brick building that housed all three businesses was an odd section of the earlier structure that was only about four feet off the ground but had the appearance of a finished rooftop—complete with shingles, exhaust vents, and ivy-covered walls with an attached steel fire escape. It was something straight out of a Technicolor Marvel monthly, just waiting for heroes to be drawn into. This was my stage, the place I spent countless afternoons, picturing myself in blue and red spandex, swinging in from an adjacent building and laying a beatdown on Doctor Octopus, all the while delivering punch lines to no one in particular. In those moments I was no longer an ordinary, awkward fourth grader who hated broccoli, geometry, and my stiff church pants—I was a webslinging, wall-crawling, wisecracking wonder, saving the day and rescuing the girl from the bad guys and the peril they generated. For a few moments after school (and several hours on the weekend) I stepped into the pages of a comic book and became the hero the planet needed. I temporarily transformed (if only in my mind) into the superhuman world-saver I wished I really was *all* the time. Having not yet been assaulted by an irradiated arachnid, I settled for the next best thing: I regularly pretended as if I had been.

I think you know what that feels like, that periodic fantasizing where you get to be more than you currently are, if only for a couple of hours. From time to time, every single one of us daydreams about being something and someone else, about transcending our ordinary selves. But what if you didn't need to borrow a fictional story for secondhand significance? What if you just needed to rewind and remember how important a story you're part of and how extraordinary you already are?

Friend, if you're breathing and your heart is working, there's a really good chance that your origin story is already in progress. Transformation is taking place, and this is super news for the hurting world you're standing on. The wild, courageous child nestled deep within you is telling you that there is still time left for you to save the day, that all is not lost, that somebody does give enough of a damn to change the outcome. And he or she is right—all is *not* lost, because you are still here and there is still time. You have 86,400 seconds in this day alone, and every single one of those small slivers of daylight is another reason to believe that you are more powerful than you realize. This is where the plot starts to twist—with you, right here, right now.

And this isn't true just for our individual journeys, but for the communities in which we live and work and worship. These dark days might be calling us all to dream again. This urgency many of us are feeling right now—this internal unrest at all that seems wrong—might be a sacred voice imploring us to entertain our latent, buried aspirations once more and to connect with like-hearted people to do the work we believe needs doing. Maybe there are muscles that we've let atrophy that we can begin to use again—compassion and generosity and creativity—in ways that we alone possess and that we can bring to bear on the rather disheartening mess in front of us, in our homes, on the news, in our neighborhoods, on our social media feeds.

I believe the daydream is still a real possibility for you, no matter how unqualified or past your prime or screwed up you feel. I know there is the remnant of a defiant hero still kicking inside you. I feel it within me, too. Four decades after my afternoon rooftop reveries, that wide-open, fearless fourth-grade boy imagining himself courageous is still residing here in the center of my chest, and every so often he rattles me alive when I lose hope. He is still aspiring to the heroic, still stumbling toward greatness, still wired to save the world and praying for hostile radioactive spiders on the back of his hand. Look down at your feet. This is the place you start. In the seconds it is taking you to read these words, you are becoming something super.

TWO

SECRET IDENTITIES AND ALTER EGOS

My friend Terri is actually a *literal* superhero. (Well, she's about as close as you can get without being able to scale walls or spin the earth backward.) During the day she's a buoyant, cheerful registered dental hygienist in Portland, Oregon, with a high school daughter and a husband of nineteen years—but on the weekends she's Rogue from Marvel's mighty X-Men or the un-flappable Batgirl. When Terri isn't diligently fighting plaque and gingivitis beneath fluorescent lights, she puts on a carefully crafted spandex costume, dons a white-streaked wig or purple cowl, and joins a dozen or so otherwise ordinary civilians in the Portland Superheroes Coalition founded by Brady Gage. These costumed crusaders travel together to children's hospitals and group homes,

giving hurting kids a chance to interact with their big-screen heroes and to have some much-needed and well-deserved joy for a
little while. After initially connecting with PSC through some kindred spirits she met during a superhero pub crawl years ago, Terri
joined the group as a way to combine her love of cosplay and comic
books with her passion for children. She is doing something that is
both simple and transformative; she identified a need and found a
unique way she could fill that void using what she loves, what she
has, and what gives her joy—which is how all ordinary superheroes
are born.

When my friend speaks of the children she crosses paths with,
it's clear that the encouragement in their interactions is reciprocal.
"Kids are so pure, the purest essence of our being," she says. "They
show emotion with no restraints from the 'real world.' They love
with the biggest hearts. Some of them have very serious health conditions, some terminal, but I have yet to visit a child who hasn't had
the strongest will to stay happy and stay strong. They truly are the
real superheroes." For Terri, the happiness she gives to other people
gets immediately passed right back, and she always leaves her time
with the children feeling lighter than when she arrived. She has her
weary eyes recalibrated and she sees the world and herself differently: both get a much-needed makeover.

In a seemingly small yet profoundly influential way, Terri is
sending powerful tremors into the world, and I'm proud to call her
a friend. She would probably tell you that what she's doing is insignificant, but it's monumental to the children she visits—and that's
the point. To them, they're not meeting a dental hygienist, they're
meeting a bona fide superhero, they're sharing space with someone

extraordinary—and the emotional lift that brings to the kids and the joyful fallout among their families and the hospital staff is beyond measure. Such opportunities exist for all of us every single day. We each have the possibility of being agents of hope and it's almost ridiculously simple: we just have to care, show up with the best of ourselves, and trust in our inherent ability to be sufficiently super. Heroes like Terri are everywhere, cleaning your teeth and waiting your tables and driving past you and sitting beside you in class—and it's really easy to miss them.

Reading *Superman* comics as a boy, I always used to marvel at the power of a pair of glasses to flummox the staff of the *Daily Planet*. For a bunch of supposedly seasoned reporters, they sure had lousy instincts—that *this* was all it took for them to miss Superman in their midst. The Man of Steel himself was actually on the payroll, passing them every day at the printer, half-heartedly singing alongside them at a coworker's awkward birthday gathering, sitting across from them at life-sucking staff meetings, and all he needed to conceal his identity was a cheap pair of Foster Grants and a fake ID. The guy was a muscle-bound, bulletproof, laser-eyed extraterrestrial, made of a nearly indestructible alloy and capable of turning the world on its very axis, but his investigative reporter coworkers couldn't recognize him in the break room, all because of some snazzy drugstore specs. (Not to mention Lois Lane's lack of awareness, but I suppose the time-tested adage *love is blind* rings true.) They somehow never saw Superman hiding within Clark Kent.

In the comics, it's funny how similar the hero and the alter ego often are, just how little outwardly separates the lowly mortals from the planet spinners. They don a pair of glasses or part their hair on the opposite side, and suddenly their greatness is buried, their true nature rendered invisible to everyone. They appear to the naked eye quite normal, while in reality being light-years from it. The audience watching this unfold on-screen gets to laugh at how unaware people are to their proximity with a world-saving demigod, and their blindness is often played for comic and ironic effect, but in real life it isn't quite as funny. In fact, there are few things more tragic than someone who is oblivious to his or her goodness and giftedness, who doesn't realize what a walking freakin' miracle they are.

We all know people who don't see in *themselves* what is so clear to others (their children, friends, coworkers, spouses), and we are as astonished at *their* blind spot as we are at that of Clark Kent's cubicle neighbors. "How can they not know how amazing they are?" we think to ourselves, but the great irony is that people are probably asking the same question about us. We're all guilty of underestimating our inherent worth, of discounting the unique arsenal of gifts at our disposal and our capacity to tangibly help the world be a more hopeful place. Though it can sometimes be a challenge to spot the greatness in our midst when it shows up in other people, it can be downright impossible to see it in the mirror. We've grown so used to our inner monologue of self-doubt and our long-simmering internalized anger that we've lost the ability to really see ourselves anymore. (When it comes to overlooking the heroic up close, Lois Lane's got nothin' on us.)

For each of us there is often a microscopic difference between our regular identities and our superselves, and the challenge we face every day is to lean toward the latter, to strain for that greatness, to aspire to what we *might* be. Much like Clark Kent's glasses, what separates us from the life we *have* and the life we *could* have is so very narrow that we'd be shocked if we realized it. Most of us are one small decision away from completely rewriting the narrative: one conversation, one relationship, or one nanosecond of fresh clarity—we just need a gentle (or sometimes forceful) nudge toward it. I'm a firm believer that in order to see something we need to see, sometimes we need a hug around the neck, and other times a kick in the behind. I'm not sure which is true for you right now, but I hope you'll receive these words in the way that most moves you, emotionally and then physically. *Movement*, after all is what we're talking about here: that sometimes infinitesimal shift in thinking or doing or spending or speaking that needs to take place in order to get us to the places we need to be and to become the people we need to become. When we *do* move, we sometimes do more than just change our circumstances; we often uncover a truer version of ourselves trapped beneath those circumstances.

I met my friend Alex a few years ago in Charlotte, just as her fifteen-year marriage was falling apart. To those of us looking on from a distance the implosion seemed sudden, but behind the scenes (to her, her two teenage boys, and others closest to her) her divorce was a final surrender following a long and brutal hidden battle. At this point, the disconnection was actually a welcome relief, that deep and teary-eyed exhale following the final ripping away of a Band-Aid that was painful but necessary for healing. The day she realized her marriage should end was a surgically precise moment of clarity that arrived after years spent enduring her husband's emotional apathy, unaddressed indiscretions, financial improprieties, and verbal assaults. The accumulation of these daily defeats had essentially rendered their relationship little more than a nearly bankrupt business partnership made of cold exchanges at the dinner table and the requisite discussion of bills and carpool responsibilities. For a while, Alex had resigned herself to believing that this was what all marriages looked like, that this was normal life. She began to view her terrible circumstances as unremarkable, and for a long time she just stopped questioning them. This is true for many of us, when for one reason or another we find ourselves acclimating to unhealthy surroundings or poisonous people or destructive behavior. Over time we slowly stop pushing back, and in the process we subjugate our true identities. We stop imagining something better or different is even an option, and we settle for the self of least resistance.

However, a few months before our meeting that day over coffee, Alex realized that not only was her marriage not normal or healthy, but that it hadn't been for a long time. As she looked back with new eyes, she understood there had been several red flags early on that she'd overlooked in her naïveté and optimism, and these unheeded warnings soon blossomed into measurable and increasingly destructive behavior shortly after her wedding. She'd taken her marriage vows seriously and wanted to hold it all together (at least for her boys, she thought), and so even with the emotional damage she was regularly sustaining, Alex endured several soul-draining years trying to salvage her relationship, trying to out-love her husband's ever-hovering demons, and waiting for the day that she would again feel that he was as invested in their marriage as she was. One morning she woke up and realized that that day was never coming. She'd reached her painful but necessary breaking point.

That afternoon as we talked, Alex unapologetically declared her emancipation from her marriage and from being hidden within it. Her confidence, her joy, and her very sense of self had been buried in that unequal partnership, and now she was excavating herself. Since the end of her marriage, as painful as it was, Alex has tapped into new capabilities as a parent, she's found her calling in a local nonprofit, and she's become far more vocal in social causes than she's ever been. When she looks in the mirror now, she sees more *Alex* than she's seen in a long time.

Maybe what you need most right now is to see yourself again, to apply new lenses that expose the obscured beauty you've been missing or become immune to. The Renaissance master Michelangelo was once asked how he created such stunning, complex figures out of massive slabs of marble. He is said to have responded, "Every block of stone has a statue inside it and the task of the sculptor is to discover it." Believing the beautiful figures were trapped in the marble until he set them free with his hammer and chisel, he would work to emancipate them from the heavy, cumbersome stone so that the world could finally see what he could see. Noticing the splendor hidden in plain sight has always been the artist's gift. Whether it's Cézanne's study of the surface of a pear, Bob Dylan's prophetic descriptions of American youth culture, or the insightful photographs of marginalized communities by Diane

Arbus—when we are allowed to view the ordinary with a fresh or different perspective, it is revelatory. We are reminded that nothing is unremarkable when it is truly seen, that there is poetry in every second, music in each unadorned moment we inhabit. Given how exhausted we all are and the ridiculous pace we usually keep, it's a herculean task to slow down enough to take note of these masterpieces woven into our otherwise mundane days, to attune our eyes to seeing them. Perhaps the most challenging act of all is spotting such greatness in ourselves. We rarely if ever entertain the idea that *we* could be the thing of indescribable beauty trapped in the stone slab, that we might be the superhuman hidden beneath some inexpensive eyeglasses. Most people I know are their own best-kept secret, always diminishing their worth, forever underestimating what they bring to the table, making the most passionate case for their unimportance and irrelevance. When we're in that headspace, we may need to hear the truth about us spoken from someone else, someone who has a vantage point we don't have. From time to time we all need others to show us what they can see in us from where they stand, attributes that we may be missing. As important, we need to be the seers, the visionaries who identify and remind people of their greatness and their goodness, so that they can get a glimpse of it and begin believing in it. We get to be the artists. We get to reveal the beauty we see buried beneath stone slabs.

My friend Morgan is a single mom, and she recently shared with me a conversation she was having with her two young daughters as they were winding up a particularly stressful day. The girls were giving her a nighttime pep talk, to which she replied, "You guys are sweet to encourage me, but if you think I have superhero powers you're gonna be disappointed when you find out I'm just a regular person." They both paused and looked at their mother for a second, and her older daughter said, "I think you have superhero *love*, Mom." Her younger daughter agreed, and the three of them embraced, with Morgan feeling incredibly moved and proud to be the person her daughters saw her to be. With a few simple words, those two small girls chipped away some of the massive stone around their mother. They saw the hero hiding in plain sight there in the living room.

I love this exchange in *Spider-Man 2*, when Aunt May offers some wise words to her superhero nephew, Peter Parker, as the two of them see a young neighbor named Henry:

HENRY JACKSON: *Hi, Peter!*

PETER PARKER: *Hey, Henry! You've grown tall.*

MAY PARKER: *You'll never guess who he wants to be . . . Spider-Man!*

PETER PARKER: *Why?*

MAY PARKER: *He knows a hero when he sees one. Too few characters out there, flying around like that, saving old girls like me. And Lord knows, kids like Henry need a hero—courageous, self-sacrificing people. Setting examples for all of us. Everybody loves a hero. People line up for them, cheer them, scream their names. And years later, they'll tell how they stood in the rain for hours just to get a glimpse of the one who taught them to hold on a second longer. I believe there's a hero in all of us, that keeps us honest, gives us strength, makes*

> *us noble, and finally allows us to die with pride, even though*
> *sometimes we have to be steady, and give up the thing we*
> *want the most—even our dreams.*

Aunt May speaks to a truth that we all understand and have experienced at one point or another: the power of another's words to crush us or propel us, the way they can completely change our trajectory in an instant. I can still remember when I was less than a year into my tenure as youth minister at my first church, a small country chapel in a pastoral Philadelphia suburb. One afternoon I was standing in the office, chatting with our church secretary, Bonnie, a kind-eyed woman with a deep, throaty laugh that she regularly launched into the ether. (Bonnie was my personally adopted Aunt May.) She was close to my grandmother's age, and though I never had a relationship with my grandmother growing up due to her battles with mental illness, Bonnie always made me feel the way I imagined most grandmothers make their grandchildren feel. She was effusive with praise and gentle with correction, and she always let me know she was in my corner when I believed that no one else was. As I was huddled over the printer while multitasking with a bit of small talk about the busy week ahead, Bonnie stopped speaking until I noticed her, looked at me, smiled widely, and said, "Son, the Holy Spirit's just drippin' off you!" How does one respond to that? I sure as heck didn't know, as you're never ready for such a lofty suggestion. Slightly embarrassed, I felt my face growing hot and I couldn't find words to reply. I just smiled back and tried not to cry on the printer paper. Bonnie was using religious language that may not resonate with you, but she was speaking something that transcends religious tradition or faith conviction. She was letting me know that she *saw* me, that she recognized something remarkable that I was oblivious to in the moment, something she thought I needed to hear and be made aware of. She did what we so need people in our lives to do: be truth-tellers who testify to our goodness so that we can realize it or be reminded of it. We all need such prophets of hope.

I may not have fully believed Bonnie's words that day and may not have known exactly how to process them in that moment, but I've never forgotten them. Two decades later, when I begin to question who I am or what I'm doing, or I find myself lacking in confidence or joy, I often remember Bonnie's affirmation spoken to me with such directness and try to see whatever it was she saw in me that day. I look for it in other people, too. I try to see it in those I cross paths with, the beautiful figure that may be trapped deep within a stone slab and hidden from view. I do my best to emancipate them from their own heads with words of truth and encouragement they deserve to hear.

Bonnie, Alex, Morgan, and Aunt May all know that we are all prone to forget who we are and to lose sight over time of our greatness. So let me remind you now, friend, in case you've forgotten or no longer can see it: You are an unqualified masterpiece. Whether you're a person who believes that life is the work of an eternal creator initiating everything, or you understand the world to be a random, organic evolutionary process—the conclusion you come to about yourself should be similarly awe-inspiring. Either you are an intentional work of art fashioned by the hand of a limitless creator, or you are a once-in-history, never-to-be-repeated miracle of matter and gravity. Either way, you are alive with possibility, deserving of reverence, and gloriously kick-ass. Don't discount your inherent goodness. Don't be your best-kept secret. Don't disguise your real identity in cheap drugstore glasses.

In the comic books, the heroes hide their true selves on purpose, often to protect those they love, to throw off the encroaching press, or to keep the bad guys at bay. It is a strategic decision of self-camouflage, usually on behalf of someone else's well-being. They have a reasonable excuse for not revealing their true identities. You and I have no such justifications for burying the best of who we are; for spending too many of our rapidly fleeting days as poorly disguised superheroes stuck on the ground pretending that we can't fly. You're staring *super* in the face every single day, and most of the time you're unaware. As we lament the sorry state of the world or the number of people who don't seem fazed by it, you and I may be missing our greatest reason to be encouraged: that there is a whole team of highly qualified world-savers out there disguised as ordinary citizens, some literally right under our noses—right there in the mirror.

KRYPTONITE AND ARCHENEMIES

An unbeatable hero makes for a pretty boring story, doesn't it? Whether in a basketball game, a movie plot, or a fictional tale, if victory is a foregone conclusion for our protagonist at the outset, it's difficult to retain our attention for very long. If there is no risk, no danger, and no true threat, there's no internal urgency and little to root for. We are drawn to those stories that tantalize us with at least the *possibility* of the hero's defeat, with the likelihood that things could quite easily go sideways and he or she might find themselves in peril. This tension is attractive to us because it allows us to see just how deep someone has to dig in order to win the day, the profound weaknesses he or she possesses, and the potential personal cost of engaging the enemy and welcoming the fight.

The allure of our idols—whether real or fictional—is that they *are* flawed, they *can* be overtaken, they *do* have clear vulnerabilities. Superman has Kryptonite and Lex Luthor; Daredevil has noise pollution and the mob boss Kingpin; LeBron James has his aging legs and the Golden State Warriors, and yet each still enters the fray and faces his own mortality or defeat on behalf of the cause— pitfall, failure, and humiliation be damned. On the field, on-screen, or in the pages of a graphic novel, these fighters inspire awe, and our reverence grows when we sense they are up against the ropes and yet still pushing toward victory, determined and undeterred. It is in this crucible of calamity that the superhero's heart is forged, and at the precipice of failure that his or her true courage is measured. We want to see people at the end of their proverbial ropes and to watch them pull themselves back with every burning muscle in them straining to do so, because the kind of visceral hope that generates in us is contagious. Flaws and villains are necessary in any good hero story, and when we're watching from a safe distance we all crave the conflict they bring with them—but the truth is, when we're walking through our own personal hell it's a lot less attractive, even if it is just as ripe with the potential for growth. In this life, facing both our limitations and our adversaries is a truly heroic act.

It's also all but unavoidable. I am sure you have a running tally of challenging people in your life. Likewise, if I asked you to name your weaknesses and imperfections, it probably wouldn't take you very long. Chances are, you have a detailed, thorough, and heavily footnoted list at the ready—possibly one handed down to you by parents, teachers, or relative strangers on the Internet and which you've committed to memory. We usually move through our days with our deficiencies and disadvantages always bouncing around in our heads, and we can zero in on them with incredible velocity and precision because we've spent a lifetime discovering, dwelling on, and magnifying them. We've also had lots of outside help in the endeavor. From an early age we're taught not to merely revel in the things we excel at, but to be ever mindful of where we are faltering. As students, we usually don't get kudos from our parents for the five classes we're acing, but there's a cautionary warning or sharp reprimand for the one that we're struggling in. (Calculus, I'm looking in your direction.) Our workplace performance reviews always begin with our stated strengths, usually to soften the blow when the inevitable supposedly "constructive" criticism comes. Our partners rarely remind us of the numerous ways we may get it right, but in spontaneous blowups they jump to alert us when we're dropping the ball.

Because of our tendency to focus on our defects, and since criticism is usually easier to offer or to absorb than praise is anyway, over time we gradually get rewired to define ourselves by our faults rather than our strengths—which is why no matter how successful or financially secure or competent we are, none of us ever feels like we have things sufficiently together in order to be what we wish we were or feel we're supposed to be or imagine that other people are. Even as highly productive, fully functioning adults, we still see ourselves as faltering, fraudulent children, not quite where we should be, perpetually not good enough, hopelessly incompetent. We live always reminded of our personal shortcomings from within and without, and as a result we spend most of our time hyperfocused on what we think we lack, fully preoccupied by our Achilles' heels— which is a shame and a waste. Such misplaced attention on our *not-quites* or *not-yets* robs us of the opportunity to embrace all that we *are* completely equipped with and perfectly positioned to do in the world. Because the truth is, our weaknesses don't define us any more than Kryptonite defines Superman. He is far more than the green, shimmering stone that is capable of sending him to his knees. Likewise, our identities are far bigger than our individual flaws. We move into superlative living when we stop apologizing for being vulnerable or beatable or unqualified and just revel in the fact that we are *all* those things and we choose to fight on anyway—that with all we lack we still can win the day.

For you this fighting might mean dusting off that dream project you shelved, launching a nonprofit, pursuing a course of study you abandoned, jettisoning an addiction, or moving toward reconciling a severed relationship. Any and all of these decisions will involve you copping to your previous failures and former frailties but flatly refusing to let them creep into the new day in front of you. Negative self-talk can be like gravity, forever pulling you down and keeping you from reaching toward the dreams you're incubating inside. Your fears and insecurities can become awfully heavy the longer you lug them around. You'll never be able to fly without letting go of the defeatist thoughts anchoring you to the ground.

Sometimes, chasing after your better self takes a deep breath and an audacious leap of faith. That was the case for Stephanie. A few years ago, she resigned from a long and lucrative newspaper career in Charlotte, North Carolina, sold nearly every possession she'd acquired, left her entire family, and headed overseas to work with the teenage children of American men and women serving in the US military in England. After a long period of personal and professional stability, surrounded by a loving assembly of family and friends, Stephanie found herself alone on an English air force base and living a completely unfamiliar daily existence, having to simultaneously adapt to a foreign culture, military life, personal upheaval, and the heavy emotional demands of caring for diverse kids in various stages of acute crisis.

When I'd Skype with Stephanie during the early years of her tenure there, I marveled at the way she had stepped almost intentionally into her weaknesses and vulnerabilities, like a storm chaser choosing to move toward the swirling funnel cloud though its hazards and ferocity were clear. As we'd talk, I'd sense her fatigue and I'd feel her frustration as she relayed all the ways she was being pressed beyond her capacity, the ways her familiar flaws were being exposed like open wounds. Yet beyond the many real and painful challenges Stephanie shared with me, what I'd hear most in her voice was the triumphant realization that despite all of it, *here she was* doing about a hundred things she'd previously convinced herself she was ill-equipped for. I could see it so clearly as I watched it all unfold, as I heard her stories. I eventually got a chance to travel overseas and witness it firsthand. She was battered and bruised and limping, but she was still saving the world for those exhausted and terrified teenagers. Had she not braved the wounds and traversed the land mines required to be there to sit across from those students, their stories would have been completely different. Before her new journey began, Stephanie could and probably would have given you a laundry list of the ways she wasn't suitable to do this work or why her personality profile would have argued for her disqualification—but she wasn't letting those things compose the narrative for her. She wasn't going to let fear be her Kryptonite, trapping her in the perceived safety of inaction. The trip across the pond hasn't been easy for my friend, but it's been abundantly fruitful, remaking her, those teenagers she loved really well, and the world you're living in right now.

It's important to remember that the presence of weaknesses doesn't make us weak, it just exposes where we're vulnerable so that we can protect ourselves, so that we can lean into our strengths, so that we can fight smarter. Like a good GPS system that helps us navigate through strange cities, awareness of our weaknesses helps us know the places we need to avoid or the spots where we're likely to get into trouble. The greatest weapon we have against our shortcomings and places of vulnerability is to know them well, to continually try to step outside ourselves and watch how we respond to stress, the way we resist or embrace change, whether we seek or shrink from conflict. A regular diet of self-reflection, along with honest feedback from loving truth-tellers and even people trained to help us better see ourselves (ministers, therapists, counselors), can fortify us in the fight to overcome our personal Kryptonite. The more you understand your entirely unique personal frailties, the better prepared you'll be when you're faced with them—and you *will* be faced with them over and over again, when you least expect them to surface. Considering your vulnerabilities and flaws now will help you prepare for when the world caves in.

Earlier I mentioned my father's sudden passing, and this was certainly a Kryptonite moment for me, an exposure to a paralyzing grief that shook me to the marrow. Since then there's been little about life that's been untouched by this tragedy, from the way the nighttime feels, to the tightening in my stomach whenever the phone rings on a Saturday morning, to the way I see my children, to the way I view the calendar. I think differently, I sense time differently, and I look at the future differently as well. But more than anything, the grief I experienced led me to a clear and startling realization: I'm not made of steel. For the past twenty years as a pastor and caregiver, I'd made a living *saving people*, dramatically flying into the burning rubble of others' lives and coming out without a scratch, carrying in my arms the grateful mortals I'd rescued. Okay, I never pictured myself in quite those grandiose terms, but I've certainly seen myself as a problem solver, a fixer, a leader, an exceptionally competent helper, and I found a good bit of my identity in those roles. I've prided myself on being professional and excellent and dependable, and maybe like you, I've been the person others come to for help in times of distress and lean on when they're overwhelmed. If there've been bullets to outrun, trains to overpower, or tall buildings to hurdle, I was at the ready—until I encountered the green stone that brought me to my knees. For the first time in my life I had to admit to other people (and to myself) that I needed saving. And for the first time, I took off the costume and the cape and stopped pretending I was so damn indestructible.

It's a pretty tough thing for any would-be hero to face weakness, to acknowledge he's reached the limit of his strength, to admit he is near defeat. I think you understand that. You may have been wearing the costume for a while yourself. You might not be an overachieving pastor, shit-stirring blogger, or rabble-rousing public speaker. Maybe you're a superstar at work or a perfectionistic parent, maybe a praiseworthy spouse or a high school sports star.

Maybe you've gained some attention or recognition or reputation by being great at something, and ever since you've become on some level a superhero. Maybe you're simply a high-functioning human being who finds your worth through the pursuit of excellence in business or physical health or material success.

The problem, is that in the same way we can find ourselves captive to our weaknesses, we can alternatively become prisoners of our proficiency, beholden to an image that is unsustainable. Lots of us manage wildly distorted pictures of ourselves, saddled with unrealistic expectations and unreasonable goals, either from outside or from within. We strain to keep it all together, to earn the accolades, to get the kudos, to look the part, to win the prize. And setting down the weight of the planet isn't easy once you're convinced that you're supposed to be carrying it, once you believe that it's solely your job to keep it all up and spinning. In fact, as a good friend once told me: "If you fancy yourself a superhero, lots of people will be more than content to wash and press your costume, point you to a phone booth, and cheer you on when you emerge." If you're exhausted from trying to be perfect, whether at home or school or in your marriage or at your job, please hear me: you can take off the costume called Perfection, because it will never fit you; it was not designed for you, and it will kill you.

And as important as admitting such truth in the mirror can be, letting others in on the news is equally critical, because it allows you to participate in authentic community with people who love you—precisely because you're not superhuman. In the wake of the loss of both my father and my illusions of being unbreakable, I was able to lean on people in ways I'd never allowed myself to, I found a vulnerability that I'd never shown, and I grew closer to the people I let carry me when I couldn't stand. Turns out it's a pretty powerful thing to admit when you feel powerless. Maybe like me, you'll need to hit some traumatic turn in your road to realize all this, but I'm hoping not. Perhaps you'll see these words as permission to be imperfect, to not have it all together, to fail and fall and cry, and maybe to be carried for a while. You don't need to fear or deny your weaknesses; you simply need to acknowledge them. Once you do, you'll be better equipped to fight those inner battles when they manifest themselves through trial or self-doubt or pessimism. But it's not just the internal skirmishes you have to brace yourself for; you also need to fortify yourself against some opposition from outside as well.

In the monumental stories we love to watch and read, it isn't only the existence of a vulnerability in the main character that draws us in; it's the presence of an archenemy, an antagonist who presents our hero with a formidable adversary, someone capable of doing tremendous harm. The Joker, Lex Luthor, Magneto—we all love a really good baddie. In fact, if we sense that the villain in a story is half-baked or unimpressive, we're usually disappointed, because we know that real resistance always produces virtue the hero couldn't unearth any other way. No one wants to see Superman fighting a nondescript, neighborhood pickpocket; we want him to face an extraterrestrial mega-monster quite capable of breaking his steel spine like a toothpick.

Life certainly imitates art with regard to our adversaries' catalytic influence on our better selves. The people who oppose us surely help define us; they spur us on to transformation. While I don't celebrate the hurtful and negative people I've met or seen from a distance, I hold some odd indirect gratitude for them, because they've often unknowingly catapulted me into spaces I'd never otherwise go and helped fashion me into the person I am as I sit here typing these words. I can mark the emotional scars they left me with, and the changes that came along with them. From Kevin and the cadre of oversize high school seniors who terrorized me when I was a freshman, to the college professor who challenged my commitment to my craft, to the egomaniacal pastor who spoke destructive words into me as a young minister, to the current malignant occupant of the Oval Office—they've each caused me to become stronger, louder, or more compassionate than I'd have been without their presence. In very specifically formative ways, each forced me to reach into a deeper reservoir and to pull out something I didn't realize was there and may never have discovered otherwise.

To lay my cards faceup on the table: I'm not the biggest fan of our current president (in case you haven't guessed by now). In fact, it's more accurate to say that the near endless list of things I prefer to him includes explosive diarrhea, root canals, and inadvertently planting my rear end in a fire ant colony. Honestly, I can imagine few people in the history of this country more responsible for a period of rapid degradation and constant urgency than the man and those he's placed around him. The fact that, as of this writing, he was placed at the helm of our nation at all is one of the sources of the greatest grief in my lifetime. And yet, I've seen the effect his tenure has had on me, and I know without a doubt that my own personal activism has been in many ways shaped as a direct response to this specific malevolence—and I'm hardly alone. Tens of millions of people marched across the world the day after the inauguration, which proved for many to be their drafting into the Resistance movement, a loosely organized collection of people committed to diversity, equality, and justice. Without such a specific and powerful threat, and without the bigotry and hatred unearthed in the process, many would never have been catalyzed into activism or propelled toward civic engagement. This is always the bad guy's odd gift to the hero in the stories we love: the villain helps our protagonist know what he stands for and what he refuses to stand for. The antagonist is invaluable in the making of the hero. Maybe you've begun to find yourself being similarly transformed by the presence of people who have come against you or criticized you or maligned you: be grateful for that. We may not welcome those who bring us pain, but in undeniable, seemingly counterintuitive ways, they perform a service to us.

The most powerful and compelling villains in the movies are so because they know the hero intimately, they understand what makes him or her vulnerable, and they can leverage those flaws to do the greatest damage. As you and I seek to be the kind of person the world needs, this presents a problem, because we will find opposition waiting for us everywhere. And paradoxically, it will be most destructive when it comes from those who have great emotional proximity to us, from the people with whom we allow ourselves to be most transparent. Our most dangerous adversaries are the ones who are on the inside; who know our hidden motives, each carefully concealed bit of pettiness and ego, every one of our secret disappointments. They know exactly what buttons to push, what vulnerabilities to attack, what words will derail. This is why we can experience such profound injury in our families and our marriages, and from the people we love dearly; because we have given them access and trust that few others have. When men and women share with me the collateral damage of their daily battles, they're almost never talking about politicians or religious leaders or faceless people off in the distance; they're telling me about the wounds inflicted by those in the room next to them or across the table from them or in photos they no longer hang in their hallways. It isn't a stranger's attacks that cause them the greatest heartache, but the friendly fire from people they believed in the most and kept the closest. This is the occupational hazard of knowing and being known.

And so here you and I stand: seeking to be super, while each day trying to overcome both our internal fragilities and our ever-present external threats, trying to fight back the demons so skillfully attacking us from our continual inner monologue, convincingly making the case for why our defeat is predetermined and our failure all but guaranteed. This could all easily overwhelm us and drive us to depression, despair, inaction, and emotional eating, or we could remember that *this* spot—the spot in the story where the hero feels fully overwhelmed and outmatched, and the seemingly unbeatable bad guy's victory is certain—is *exactly* where things get really good. When we see our protagonists driven to their knees, their brows furrowed and their lungs bursting while everything goes to hell around them, we don't lose hope, because we know we're about to see what Kryptonite and master criminals can't measure or defeat: the fierce and furious heart of a superhuman.

FOUR

UTILITY BELTS AND ARMOR SUITS

*B*atman is known for his utility belt, a seemingly inexhaustible source of gadgets and gizmos that often appear tailor-made to extricate him from the most impossible of calamities. This was used to hilarious effect during Adam West's campy sixties TV tenure, during which the titular figure never seems to want for *just* what he needs at any given moment of threat. In one memorable episode, while hanging from a helicopter and half engulfed by a persistent great white, Batman famously manages to retrieve a can of shark repellent—because what proper superhero living in the heart of a major metropolitan area wouldn't have such necessities?

In Tim Burton's 1989 *Batman* movie, the Joker (played with maniacal glee by Jack Nicholson) watches the Caped Crusader rocketing skyward from his minions' clutches via a grappling hook gun while clutching a stunned Kim Basinger. With unapologetic wonder, Nicholson's Joker asks aloud, "Where does he get those wonderful toys?" Bruce Wayne's collection of "toys" was certainly the result of time and trial and came at considerable cost. His utility belt, much like everything in his seemingly inexhaustible arsenal of weaponized vehicles and Batcave accoutrements, was the product of the long and meandering path he'd walked. He'd witnessed his parents' murder, stumbled to find purpose in his opulent but lonely life, diligently honed his combat skills, and wrestled with the rage from watching evil people destroying his beloved city. Bruce Wayne didn't just wake up one day and *choose* to be Batman. He became the hero Gotham City needed in microscopic increments over many years, filling his superhero storehouse along the way as he realized what he had and what he lacked in order to face the bad guys and save the day.

You have an extraordinary utility belt in *your* possession as well, a sprawling assortment of disparate tools you've acquired over time. Your natural abilities and life experiences, your specific personality traits and the way you're wired all comprise the singular arsenal you have access to—and it is a game changer. On days when the world is low on hope, this is how you can make your indelible mark: by simply drawing from the wealth at your disposal and doing what only you are equipped to do. Just like our comic book idols, our greatest heroes in music, politics, social justice, or our families aren't created in a vacuum or an instant. They are defined and redefined by their surroundings and experiences and relationships. People who change the world aren't remarkable until they are called by circumstances to be remarkable. As is true of our favorite caped comic book deities, they are the product of the specific path they've walked, because that path has yielded someone unprecedentedly qualified to be a rescuer, a helper, and a healer.

So, yes, you may look around at the state of the world or the state of your marriage or the condition of your family and feel as though the situation is dire. From where you're standing it all might well appear to be a hot, steaming shit show being live tweeted by the president. But *that* fact isn't worth dwelling on (unless, of course, you determine yourself capable of spinning the planet backward and undoing all the already-done stuff, and that would be a feat for even the most super of superheroes). The *only* question worth entertaining when faced with the daily disasters and dumpster fires outside the window or on your newsfeed or in your home or in your head is, "What am I going to do about it?" And answering that question has destiny-shifting potential, because unquestionably and without any hyperbole whatsoever *whatever* you decide to do has never before been done in quite the way you will do it, with your particular set of tools and your specific amalgamation of gifts. However you choose to respond to everything that feels wrong in the world, it will be an historic occasion. Because your life is a novel presence here, what you bring to the table is always a revelation, even if it feels wholly ordinary and not the least bit noteworthy to you. You may dismiss such lofty talk or conclude that your contributions (as well-meaning as they might be) amount to very little in the big picture, but you would be terribly mistaken. Your utility belt isn't to be dismissed or underestimated; it's to be wielded unapologetically like the well-earned, precision weapon against hopelessness that it is.

The fact is, you're made out of the same raw material that everyone who ever inspired or encouraged you from a distance is made of. Just like Bono or Oprah or Bill Gates or Barack Obama. Like every world-class surgeon, influential artist, audacious activist, or brilliant scientist, you, too, are an original cocktail of matter held together by gravity and 1.5 millimeters of flesh. You are comprised of the same *stuff* as the stars and the wildflowers and the butterfly wings. Who are you to declare yourself incapable of comparable brilliance? How dare you diminish your very specific capacity to be who the world needs, when you're right here, fully able to be exactly that? Revolutions have always been initiated by regular folks who've simply shown up in the mundane space of their unspectacular days, done what they could, and hoped that it made a dent—and, friend, it always makes a dent.

Natalie Weaver understands a bit about showing up and doing what you can with the tools at your disposal (and the ones you aren't even aware you're carrying around). The North Carolina mother of three didn't set out to be an activist—she just wanted to be a mom. For as long as she could remember, having a big family was the dream she most cultivated in her heart. Nine years ago that dream came true with the arrival of Natalie and her husband Mark's first child, Sophia. However, the Weaver family's origin story would prove to be very different than the one the young couple had always pictured prior to that day. Sophia was born with Rett syndrome, along with another undiagnosed condition, which together rendered her unable to speak, walk, or take care of herself. With severe deformities to her face, hands, and feet, Sophia has already endured nearly two dozen surgeries and countless daily, painful obstacles in her young life. From the very first moment Sophia arrived, Natalie became something she didn't realize she was capable of being before that: she became a *fighter*, caring for her daughter, advocating loudly for her, and learning to navigate the intricate, convoluted maze of the American health-care system in order to make sure Sophia had every chance to survive and to weather her formidable and life-threatening physical challenges. Sophia's life became Natalie's cause, the center of her new personal activism. That task alone, paved with as much adversity as it was, was certainly enough of a burden—and yet two years into her exhausting journey, when North Carolina politicians announced a plan to severely reduce services to medically fragile children like Sophia, she found life inviting her into more. With two other moms, Natalie launched a small Facebook support group to serve as home base for other parents with physically vulnerable kids. It would serve as the hub for their fight to defeat the proposed state funding cuts. Natalie recalled the pivotal plot twist moment, when with some hesitation she typed out a message to the other moms: "I'll do whatever it takes to help." It would soon be apparent that what it would take, was someone to be a public presence, an out front, vocal mouthpiece willing to speak to the media, testify in political hearings, and be the visible face of their efforts—all things Natalie never imagined herself doing. It was, as she said, "the one thing I *didn't* want to do." For a while she waited to step forward, hoping another person would appear and volunteer, someone better equipped or more experienced, yet all the while reiterating to the other moms, "If no one will do it, I'll do it."

As often happens with superhero origin stories, sooner or later the heroes realize that *they* are the people they're waiting for—that this is their specific invitation to become something bigger than they believed themselves prepared or qualified for. Natalie stepped out into a new and terrifying space, fueled by a compassion for families in trauma that far outweighed the internal fear. Accessing reservoirs of empathy and strength that she didn't even realize were there, Natalie embraced her new calling as a very public advocate. She was still fighting—now, not only for Sophia, but also for thousands of children and their families who were similarly imperiled and overwhelmed. After securing a victory in their effort to preserve state funding in North Carolina, Natalie and the two moms she began this advocacy journey with realized that this was more than a momentary need; it was a perennial one. Understanding that they had been brought together not for an event but for something far more enduring, the moms launched a nonprofit called Advocates for Medically Fragile Kids NC, and for the past two years they've been on the front lines of the seemingly endless battles to secure care for the most vulnerable in North Carolina and beyond.

Natalie discovered gifts she was oblivious to, specific abilities that were unearthed simply because they were needed in that moment, and it seemed no one else would show up with them. In the same way, our tool belts will sometimes be assembled as we follow passions and hone skills that either come naturally to us or give us joy (artistic ability, an outgoing personality, an entrepreneurial mind, or great attention to detail). Other times, the needs and crises around us will create opportunities to discover hidden resources, heretofore not yet mined. In those moments of urgency, we'll look at a situation and see a gap in leadership or a lack of volunteers or a technical need or a place of pain, and without knowing whether or not we're capable of remedying the situation, we'll step forward. When we do (either suddenly or gradually), we often discover that we have exactly what is needed for the time and place we find ourselves in. And we'll discover that the gifts we use for goodness' sake have a way of multiplying beyond what we ever imagined when we began.

Natalie's journey of self-discovery reminds us that underestimating our contributions is easy to default to, especially while we're standing still, counting all the reasons we aren't the person required. However, once we push through the inaction of doubt and actually *move*, we realize how capable and prepared we actually are or can become over time, through work and challenge. Don't wait until you feel confident or comfortable or deserving enough to do whatever it is you dream of doing or believe needs doing. Those moments are few and far between. Instead, take *some* sort of action now, and trust that on the other side of the risk and insecurity and the initial stumbles, will come the revelation that your life always has more surprises to give.

It's important to remember that your tool belt isn't just the stuff you can do or the tasks you perform—it's *who you are*, your particular presence. All too often, most of us fail to properly recognize or value what makes us unique and see it as an advantage. When actress and writer Lena Waithe accepted the 2017

Emmy Award for her work on the Netflix series *Master of None*, she offered this encouragement to members of the LGBTQIA community: "The things that make us different, those are our superpowers. Every day when you walk out the door and put on your imaginary cape and go out there and conquer the world, because the world would not be as beautiful as it is if we weren't in it." Waithe's stirring declaration is one every human being would be wise to embrace regardless of identity, orientation, or any other qualifier—and it is in fact the wild, pulsating message at the heart of this book: you *are* made of super stuff. It's not hyperbole, it's simply how it is.

Think about the people right now whom you admire and respect and want to emulate, those you recognize as game changers, as catalytic leaders, as planet rockers, and I'll guarantee something is categorically true of them: none of them ever feel fully deserving of the accolades they receive. They're always battling self-doubt, depression, and their own ever-present weaknesses and idiosyncrasies. The very abilities and contributions that inspire you and give you encouragement and spur you on in difficult days, are likely things they've written off or undervalued before. Without exception, every single one of them has stood where you now stand: wondering if they mattered and if they had anything worthwhile to give and feeling fairly certain they didn't. They, too, likely doubted the catalytic power of their story and the resonance of their voice. This is one of the core truths in this superhuman story: ordinary is a myth. Ordinary is a lie we tell ourselves to avoid failure. Ordinary is an excuse we make for not being braver. There is no magic to the lives we recognize as extraordinary. It isn't smoke and mirrors and wand-waving spells. It's about presence and sweat and time, about getting up every single day and doing the usually unglamorous work of living well and giving of ourselves and trusting that it will produce fruit over time, even when it looks quite fruitless in the moment.

You may be thinking this all sounds great, but you're not quite sure what *your* hope-bringing arsenal of "gadgets and gizmos" actually is. This might be a good time to take a tool belt inventory by reflecting on the following questions:

WHAT CAN YOU DO? You have practical, tangible gifts: talents to create, write, cook, build, fix, develop, etc. Right now there are places those skills are in short supply and there are people who could benefit from them in countless ways. Find these places and these people and begin making your mark.

HOW DO YOU THINK? The ways you solve problems, resolve conflict, and approach challenges are all completely unique to you. Your mind works very differently than that of anyone around you, and for that reason you can generate ideas and refine systems and build relationships that no one else can.

WHAT ARE YOUR RESOURCES? You have access to a treasure trove of valuable raw material that you can leverage in the cause of goodness: financial capital, buildings and gathering spaces, business partnerships, and equity of trust in the community. How can you spend or share your wealth to fill in the gaps you see in the world?

HOW ARE YOU WIRED? Think about your personality. Are you gregarious or thoughtful, bold or gentle, fearless or cautious? Do you naturally take the lead or thrive behind the scenes? Either way, these attributes uniquely qualify you to do what no one else on the planet can do.

WHAT IS YOUR CIRCLE OF INFLUENCE? Your friendships, business networks, social media platforms, and family relationships all form a unique imprint. If you could engage all of those people for a cause or a movement, what would it be? What would you ask of them, say to them, invite them to do? When you have an answer to that question—ask it, say it, invite them.

I hope you're beginning to realize that you have a slew of necessary tools in tow right now, and that you're beginning to dream of how and when you might use them in order to create the world you'd like to see. But be prepared, as you do this planetary remodeling, you may find yourself needing protection from the people who'd rather you do nothing and keep your mouth shut.

Tony Stark is Iron Man, the erstwhile leader of the Avengers and a guy who's no stranger to courageous, universe-saving work, though without his high-tech suit of armor he is decidedly more vulnerable to catastrophic injury and death than many of his caped colleagues. In fact, given the scale and ferocity of his enemies and the blows he sustains engaging them, it's safe to say he wouldn't have made it to a sequel without it. The suit protects him from attack, it shields him from the elements, and it exponentially multiplies his strength. Tony is surely far more than the suit, of course, but that suit allows him to be his best by toughening up his exterior so he can brave the perils he faces. He isn't bulletproof, so he needs to wear an exterior that is.

You aren't bulletproof either, friend. No matter how capable or talented you are, if you're going to do heroic work here in the world, you're going to have to develop a protective layer around yourself, too, a way of shielding your heart from the conflicts and the criticisms that come, so that these things don't do you in prematurely. If there's a common thread running through the people I meet in my travels lately, it's exhaustion. A huge portion of the population of this planet is thoroughly depleted—physically, emotionally, and spiritually—because the accumulation of sadness and stress has exceeded their capacity to endure it. We can all weather pushback and fatigue in small bursts for a short time, but to sustain ourselves for the long haul to do a lifetime of world-saving work without losing our minds and breaking our bodies, we need more than adrenaline, wine, and chocolate. Whether in matters of activism or career or parenting, many well-meaning, deeply feeling people burn out because they allow the storms around them and inside of them to consume them. If you aren't actively working to prevent it, the bad news and the harsh words and the mean people will get inside your system and create a toxic environment in which hope cannot survive. Just as your utility belt of talents, burdens, and passions is fully unique to you, the fashioning of your protective armor suit will be similarly personalized—but here are a few ideas that may be helpful in fortifying yourself for the fight:

1. **REMEMBER WHO YOU ARE.** Identity is at the core of self-protection: being able to differentiate between *you* and

the things people think and say about you. Too many ordinary heroes succumb to defeat or conflict when they allow their critics and adversaries to define them. I've often said that if hell exists, it will look a lot like a blog comments section, and early in my journey as a public figure I regularly found myself either morose or furious because of the hateful and demeaning words people addressed to me. It took me a while to realize I didn't have to accept delivery, to remind myself that those commentators were operating with incomplete information about me, so I needn't believe their words as gospel. This isn't just true of online trolls either. No one around you really knows you fully, so refuse to let anyone—not a boss or a family member or a spouse or a former friend—tell you who you are. When you know who you are, you make it much more difficult for people who assume they can define you.

2. ***TRANSFORM THE NEGATIVITY.*** In Marvel's blockbuster *Black Panther*, the titular hero, T'Challa, has an energized suit of interactive metal designed by his tech mastermind sister, Shuri. One of the suit's major upgrades from previous film iterations is its ability to capture and store kinetic energy and then release it when needed. As bullets and body blows strike the suit, they actually strengthen it. T'Challa is able to take everything his enemies throw at him over time and respond to it in one powerful, redemptive act of resistance. This is how you can save the world and save yourself at the same time: by taking every vicious attack,

every hateful diatribe, every improperly ascribed motive and letting it fuel your activism and reinforce your character. In practical terms, that simply means that rather than meeting someone's cruelty with direct opposition (an online adversary, a corrupt politician, a manipulative friend, an antagonistic coworker), you channel that cruelty into measurable work elsewhere that makes the world less cruel. Or instead of allowing the lack of compassion you encounter in the world to seep into your heart and weigh you down with a crippling despair, you find a way to tangibly make the world more compassionate through acts of service, and you find hope in the way that you're tipping the scales from enmity to love.

3. ***WITHDRAW FROM THE FRAY.*** Every hero needs a rest. Superman retreats to his Fortress of Solitude, Batman sits fireside at stately Wayne Manor, and Wonder Woman rests on the shoreline cliffs of Themyscira. You need to regularly step away from the noise and conflict to recharge your body and recalibrate your brain; to find a place to be still and silent and have your magnified threats right-sized again. Part of developing a good defense system is knowing that you can't always be in the fight. Sometimes you have to pause the world-saving work and do whatever it is that brings you peace and gives you life, whether that means taking time to meditate or exercise, grabbing a nap at the park, calling up a friend for lunch, or lying on the grass and feeling yourself exhale fully. This is the two-step dance of engaging and withdrawing.

My friend Natalie seems to have found a way to build her suit of armor. With all the legislative battles and the press conferences and the keynote speeches she has logged doing advocacy work, at the end of the day she is still a mom. That was the first dream, and Sophia is her first dream child. Being a mother is still her greatest passion, and the toll of being a parent in such adverse conditions weighs heavily on her. The fear she has for Sophia is constant, the health threats ever-present, and the emotional wounds she and Mark receive because of other people's seemingly endless capacity for cruelty toward their daughter is draining. But like Tony Stark's or T'Challa's suits of armor, this sustained damage forms protective calluses that fortify them and enable them to keep fighting. It clarifies why they do this work, and it allows them to become ever stronger even as the adversity grows. What becomes clear when talking with Natalie is that she has what so many on-screen and ordinary superheroes have: a defiant spirit that refuses to yield to the circumstances, no matter how intimidating or painful or dire they become. She is being the kind of person the world needs because she's felt that need herself and decided she isn't content with anyone else walking that road alone. When I ask Natalie where she finds joy amid it all, she tells me that it is in those quiet moments when she and Mark and her children are all together in their home, when Sophia is not in acute distress, when her body is peaceful, when they are simply a family. In that stillness is the dream. These moments nourish her and fuel her to go back out every day and do all the things that she never thought she could do—and now must do: fight for people because they deserve someone fighting for them.

Friends, your previous struggles, disappointments, victories, and failures have constructed the fully customized tool belt around your waist, preparing you to make your specifically heroic contribution to the planet in this moment. Your specifically meandering road has uniquely equipped you with an arsenal of weapons to bring into the battle for a more just and decent world. Not only that, but as you step into the tumult, as you push past the fear and decide to do the things that you once wished someone else would do—you find those hidden, untapped resources that will carry you even further, protecting you from physical deterioration and emotional breakdown.

The scar tissue of your prior defeats isn't just wasted pain: it is the very armor that shields you presently, making you stronger than you'd have been had you not weathered such things. The calluses caused by time logged here on the planet could be cause for bitterness if you fail to appreciate them—or they can become the buffer that protects you as you fight on. Whether you feel like you're fully entrenched in the planet-changing work you were made for or just tiptoeing toward it, whether you have a clear calling or you're simply looking to walk into a better version of yourself, this is a good time to inventory your utility belt and take stock of the assortment of gadgets and weapons you bring to the table in the fight to save the world. I'm guessing it's a bounty.

PART TWO

ORDINARY SUPERPOWERS

What kind of people does the world need right now? I bet if we asked that question to a group of disparate people from all across the planet, we'd find great affinity in their responses, commonalities that transcend political affiliation, religious tradition, age, race, gender, orientation, nation of origin, or income level. If we listen closely to people, both those we know intimately and those we see from a great distance, we'd discover that we largely value many of the same things and lament the same gaps in the world. It turns out that there is more agreement on the best way to be human than we usually think, far more than our divisive forces (in media, politics, or religion) would suggest. *This* is where hope lies—in those universally shared values, those common aspirations, those ordinary superpowers that we can cultivate in order to begin crafting a global revolution alongside like-hearted people. Imagine what the world would be like if we spent every day aspiring to be our most generous, kindest, most compassionate selves. It would be a far more hospitable place for people, strewn with far less loneliness, pain, and grief. So let's start there, by cultivating the transcendent, universally treasured traits that will help us become a bit better at being human, because better humans make for a better humanity.

"THE SAFEST HANDS ARE STILL OUR OWN."

—CAPTAIN AMERICA

COMPASSION

There are all sorts of superheroes out there: those who stay in the shadows, working clandestinely under the cover of night, and those who step fully into daylight, making their presence boldly known. Some are stealthy and understated, others brash, with a penchant for the dramatic. There are world-savers who exuberantly embrace their destiny, and others who barely keep a tenuous peace with it. In the comic book mythos we find a diverse assortment of characters: angry heroes, wisecracking heroes, grim-faced heroes, and idealistic heroes—we just don't find many apathetic heroes. There is a defining characteristic shared by all the wonder women and super men who fill pages and multiplex screens: they all vehemently give a damn. It's exhausting to give a damn these days, isnt it?

The word *compassion* has its original roots in the word *bowels*. It was once believed that our deepest emotions and vital organs both inhabited the same space in our bellies, that we could feel so deeply witnessing another's pain as to become internally disturbed to the point of sickness. This is why it's not inaccurate when we say today that someone's story of suffering *moves* us. With that phrase, we're expressing that visceral solidarity with another person that reaches down into the very core of who we are, as we imagine someone's specific discomfort and endeavor to alleviate it. That philosophy of *stepping into the shoes* of another is at the center of most faith traditions and moral codes; it is the gilding around the Golden Rule. And though such vicarious distress on behalf of another is an incredible gift, it's becoming more and more rare—and in fact is often treated by some as a weakness. In political discourse and online conversation, the descriptor *bleeding heart* is tossed out like an insult, as if feeling deeply or being burdened by someone else's plight is a character flaw. Somehow the empathetic spirit we treasure in our comic book movie heroes that causes them to brave monsters and mortar fire, is treated in real life as something to be embarrassed about or apologize for. In a culture that's become more and more apathetic and increasingly oblivious to others' pain, deep feelers are viewed as oddities, emotionally unstable sideshow freaks who cry easily and prematurely wilt in the face of adversity—snowflakes. You might be feeling similarly apologetic about your own unusual capacity to give a damn, as if this is somehow a deficiency. Don't be fooled for a minute, friend: your compassion isn't a shortcoming; it is the greatest of day-saving, despair-fighting superpowers. The world needs joyful, defiant damn-givers.

Anna Marie (aka Rogue) is one of my favorite members of the X-Men, a team of young mutants imbued with unusual abilities that cause them great turbulence. Anna's superhuman gift is the ability to touch people and to instantly absorb their memories and feel their feelings. On the surface it seems like a rather unremarkable power when compared with the far sexier capabilities of invisibility, weather manipulation, or being able to toss a tank over one's head. In fact, Anna spends much of her young life resenting her abilities, believing them to be a curse. For her, stepping inside another's skin is usually no picnic, as she gazes upon things she'd much rather not see and has to walk through a hell she'd just as soon have avoided.

The same is true for us here in the lesser realms, where we who practice empathy understand the tremendous strain of realizing someone else's burden and feeling the responsibility to move like a foolhardy storm chaser toward it. We know the emotional toll that kind of work can take on the human heart. For Rogue, empathy comes involuntarily. She doesn't have to try—she is hit upon contact by an immediate and disorienting flood of feelings, thoughts, memories, and desires. They're all downloaded into her body in an instant, and avoiding them is all but impossible. We mortals have to work a lot harder to care that deeply. We can't simply place a hand on someone's shoulder and suddenly understand him or her, or engage in some cursory, drive-by empathy and imagine it is correctly informed. We need to slow down, to spend time with people, to get close enough and linger long enough to learn their stories. Real compassion comes from taking the time and the care to listen— really listen—and offer sustained, steady attention to the needs of another. Most of us don't allow for such inconvenient interruptions to our schedules. The velocity and crowded nature of our daily calendars make such attentiveness nearly impossible.

Speed, it turns out, is compassion's great Kryptonite. When we are living so overscheduled, so scattered, and so immersed in the busyness of life and the manufactured urgency of social media, we don't feel we have the time to sit with other people's stories or their pain long enough to truly feel its weight. Their plight never gets a chance to reach the center of our bellies and to internally disrupt us to the point of compassionate movement. In fact, we are so completely saturated every day with suffering, that it now takes something monumentally tragic or incredibly close to home to move us. Thanks to a perpetual, almost hourly news cycle that thrives on escalating catastrophe and emotional emergency, we've built up a dangerous tolerance to everyday human suffering, and as a result, more and more hurting people are becoming invisible to us. They're being forced to compete for our attention with breaking news and trending names and presidential Twitter rants—and they're losing.

That said, most people wake up every day trying to be decent human beings. I'm sure you do. When we hear about tragedy befalling people, when we witness their injury, when we have injustice placed in our path, we almost always feel bad—at least momentarily. Our initial knee-jerk empathetic response is fairly universal, common to people of every political affiliation and religious tradition. The problem is that for too many people this often feels like enough. The suffering of another registers a twinge of sadness and a brief change of countenance, and we count *that* in itself as virtue. In other words, we feel good about ourselves for feeling bad. We might drop a sad face emoji in someone's timeline or say we're praying for them or sending positive thoughts. We then return to our lives already in progress, relatively unaffected and having made little effort to tangibly impact the situation, yet feeling the inner satisfaction of having cared. We may not do anything beyond that moment to alleviate the person's pain or change his dire circumstances, but we pat ourselves on the back, giving ourselves credit for a modicum of empathy.

Imagine this scene playing out in a Batman movie: It opens with Bruce Wayne sequestered in the bowels of the Batcave, surveying a wall of monitors displaying the streets of his beloved Gotham. Suddenly his eyes squint to focus and his jaw tightens, while the Joker and his henchmen pop out of a parade float and begin spraying the crowd with a curling wave of thick, green gas. As people begin gasping for air, clutching their throats and falling to the ground, the Joker cackles with abandon. From the other side of the screen we see Bruce Wayne clearly overwhelmed and distressed by the horror he is witnessing, as the Bat Signal streaks across the night sky. We're certain he's about to don the cape and cowl and board the Batmobile toward the city, but instead he turns off the monitor and walks away, raiding the Bat pantry for some emotional eating and telling Robin about the horrible thing he just saw and then binge watching a new season of his favorite drama—end of scene. We'd rightly conclude that he's a pretty lousy superhero. We expect him to do more than just give a damn—we expect him to give a damn enough to *do* something.

Many times we stop at initial empathy, never arriving at

compassionate activism—not because we're lazy or selfish or callous, but because we don't know exactly what to do about the horror we're witnessing. We allow the overwhelming suffering around us to freeze us into complacency, mistakenly believing we aren't equipped for whatever might be required beyond the momentary sadness we feel. We see something terrible happen and we wait, believing some later clarity will rouse us out of inaction. But heroic endeavors usually don't work that way. We almost never have the information we think we need before we move toward suffering. The moving itself brings us closer to pain, and *that* proximity begins filling in the gaps of our understanding and tells us what to do next. For example, you hear this whenever there's a news story about someone saving another person from the burning wreckage of a car or plucking them from an overflowing river or stopping a carjacking. The spontaneous heroes rarely have time to consider the options or prepare a proper response or inventory their skill sets to determine whether they're qualified—their empathy, their availability, and the peril of another human qualify them. They are moved to move, and it is *that* heart-driven, urgency-created activity that saves other imperiled souls from burning buildings, raging waters, and masked assailants. It isn't the concern alone that brings rescue, but people propelled by that concern into the troubled person's path. The news story heroes all say the same thing: "I just did what anyone else would have done." But we know this isn't true. Everyone feels, but not everyone *moves*. Empathy without action isn't much help. We need to become action figures.

My good friend George is a compassionate superhuman. I can tell this not because he often asks me how I'm doing. Lots of people do that: friends, neighbors, hotdog vendors, people I pass on the street who make eye contact. I know George is uniquely empathetic because after asking the question, he waits for an answer. He looks me in the eye and he listens intently. He endures the carefully re-hearsed, knee-jerk response I give him ("Things are good.") and he asks me (sometimes invasive) follow-up questions. He doesn't let me off the hook when I try to fake him out by pretending I'm fine, when I offer up the default response without thinking. He's adept at weeding through my superficial bullshit to reach the wounds I'd much rather keep hidden. This kind of loving intrusion is a real gift, and so are those who practice it. People, probably even you, are longing for this, for others to lean in long enough and listen carefully enough to overcome our best efforts at camouflaging our wounds. Most of the time we ask people how they are, we really don't want honesty, because that comes with burdens that can prove heavy to carry. We're usually pressed for time (or imagine we are) and not interested in an answer that will derail our plans or take us off our stride or slow us down with messy information about the marital implosions and medical detonations people are deal-ing with. We certainly don't want to have to jump into the jagged trenches with them as they're suffering, but this is what compas-sionate superheroes do: they seek the truth about people's hearts and they feel compelled to act, despite the risk of inconvenience and the change of plans required.

My work as a minister is predicated on my emotional eyesight,

on continually scanning the horizon and looking for those concealed aches out there, the hidden chronic pain all people feel but
try to keep hidden from view. I try to listen deeply, to look carefully, and to gently unearth the suffering buried beneath the surface. Each day I cultivate empathy and practice compassion as my
life's work—but I'm not alone. This is a universal calling. These
caring practices aren't reserved for clergy or spiritual leaders, and
they aren't relegated to churches, mosques, or temples. Wherever human beings can be found, great pain is sitting there with
them—and so, too, is the need for someone to alleviate that pain.
Regardless of your occupation, background, or any other qualifiers, you have the same opportunity and ability to step into other
people's stories in wonderfully redemptive ways, to be an agent of
compassion.

This is the gift we can give a world filled with hurting people:
our time and attention, our willingness to engage with an open
heart. Though the way we move in response to the suffering outside our windows will be wholly original, it all begins with what I
like to call the Art of Not Looking Away, that refusal to turn from
the pain in our path. We've all had the experience of passing someone broken down on the side of the road, feeling the prompt to
stop, and then, for whatever reason, continuing on. We often feel
tension in the moment, rationalizing why we couldn't or shouldn't
have pulled over, and assuring ourselves that someone will come
along and help those we drove by. We may initially feel guilt at
our inaction, though that tends to dissipate once the strangers get
smaller in our rearview mirror. Being a person of compassion means
not assuming that someone else is coming. It means resisting the

temptation to walk, drive, or scroll past news that is unpleasant or frightening. It means leaning in instead of turning away when you encounter someone suffering. After all, it's likely that anywhere you place your feet, there are people living as tortured ghosts, aching in silence and solitude because their pain is overlooked or because others choose to avoid the inconvenience of *seeing* that hurt.

Some measure of compassion is common to all of us, part of a kind of "base package" of our humanity, albeit limited and incredibly selective. Every one of us cares deeply about some people, with those closest to us meriting our greatest urgency, a circle that expands from our immediate families, to our extended families, then our friends, our colleagues, our communities and towns, and beyond that to those we feel an affinity for because of nationalism or religion or worldview. The closer proximity we have to people, the more we seem to be moved when they are threatened. Regardless of our religious upbringing, social status, or political leanings, we all understand that kind of selective empathy rooted in self-preservation. Even the most diabolical of supervillains has a reservoir of compassion for his own loved ones, if not anyone beyond that— a fact that ironically often serves as the impetus for his unhinged efforts to destroy humanity.

I had just finished a speaking event recently when a woman in the audience came to talk to me about the people she views as her adversaries across the aisles of religion and politics. "Deep down," she said, "all parents want the same thing for their kids: for them to be healthy and happy and safe."

I knew what she was trying to say, and I admired this attempt to find common ground that even the most ardent enemies may share—the love of their children. But most decent human beings love and want to care for their children. The desire to protect our own is a hardwired brain feature built on millions of years of protection and survival instincts. It's certainly noble, but it isn't all that virtuous. Paradoxically, this natural impulse explains the rising tribalism we find ourselves in; people hunkered down in heavily fortified bunkers alongside those they deem "their people," whether based on race or religion or nation of origin or political affiliation. This highly selective, self-serving compassion is the very heart of *America First*. It's the foundation of a border wall. It's the reason someone applauds ICE raids or travel bans, or opposes free lunch programs or universal health care: they don't want someone else to have something they have. The fierce nationalism and rising hostility toward marginalized communities on display in America is the fruit of a toxic selfishness that compels people to hoard resources, opportunity, and benefits, for fear they will be left without. And often that's done with the rationalization of "protecting" one's children and family.

And so right now, the real battle isn't between good people and bad people—it's between openhanded people and closefisted people. Poised on either side of the debate in matters of education and health care and faith and immigration aren't people who love their children and people who don't—but people who love all children, and those who care only for their own. We need to love wider and further.

Of course it makes perfect sense to be burdened for the safety and happiness of those we consider our tribe: our children, our spouses, the people we live and work closely alongside. This all feels quite normal, and yet the challenge (and opportunity) is to feel as deeply for humanity as a whole, for the planet, for the welfare of strangers.

I am inviting you to this wider, deeper affection, because it's something the world desperately needs right now. We need ordinary heroes who are as profoundly burdened by suffering off in the distance as that occurring at arm's length, who have a love for people that transcends faith tradition, political affiliation, or national border. In a world that is ever more segmented by tribalism, we need people whose empathy reaches across those superficial divides and embraces the breadth of humanity. These practitioners of compassion are able to see a child across town, or on the other side of the country, or halfway around the world as inherently valuable as the one in their nursery.

But this work is hazardous on the human heart. If you are such a person or aim to be such a person, these are incredibly treacherous times, because there is so very much to be grieved by. It is a perilous act, simply waking and reaching for your phone and wading into the relentless flood of things capable of breaking a heart. This steady stream of bad news can easily overwhelm those who suffer vicariously, and while others seem quite capable of shutting it all out and resuming normal life, you aren't, because this *is* your normal. It is your default setting to give a damn, and so for you to try to stifle this impulse is to be less than the truest true of who you are; it is to bury the best of you. To do so would be an act of personal treason. The great problem with affixing one's heart to one's sleeve is that people who don't normally feel deeply in this way aren't equipped to understand the toll these days take on you. They aren't capable of comprehending the despair that accompanies daily life, the compounding heaviness that builds with each boldface headline, with every breaking story, with each graphic video. I suppose I could help you lessen the severity of this internal burden, but honestly I'm not interested in that, in making you less compassionate. Many people might advise you not to care as much as you do, but I won't, as I know the impossibility and the insult of the ask. I know that this is simply who you are; it's how your heart works. More than that, I know that this treasure—this incredible, counterintuitive ability to truly *feel*—is an invaluable gift to the world, and it is more precious now than ever. When so many are pushed past the threshold of their empathetic capabilities by the circumstances, we need resilient hearts that can continue to open themselves to wounding on behalf of others. That, after all, is what compels our on-screen heroes to head toward calamity when so many others understandably run the other way. And like all treasures, it is costly. This deep empathy comes with sacrifice and sorrow, and that's something you're going to have to live with, the same way those oversensitive to ultraviolet rays need to prepare for twelve or so hours of sunlight each day. Yes, you need to guard yourself from too much exposure, to shield yourself at times; you need to step away often so that you are not irreparably damaged by the environment and the effect it has on you. That is perhaps the greatest danger for those of us who feel deeply: not becoming compassionate martyrs, not being destroyed by our own hearts, not becoming so consumed by suffering that we succumb to it.

But, friend, in these days when it is tempting to be apathetic and to turn inward and to say "to hell with it all," the world needs the damn-givers, good people who refuse to surrender to the bad news or the bad guys, who will not become hardened beyond the capacity of caring. It needs heroic human beings who still run headlong into the fray, bleeding hearts affixed to their sleeves, those with just enough hope to believe others are worth sacrificing for, crying for, fighting for, bleeding for. It needs you.

SIX

"WE HAVE TO GIVE UP THE THING WE WANT THE MOST."

—MAY PARKER

SACRIFICE

Being a superhero really has to put a strain on one's social life. What do you do when you're about to sit down to the most perfectly cooked porterhouse on the planet, across from someone you've waited months to see, and out of the corner of your eye you notice the Bat Signal piercing the evening skyline? What happens when you're gathered with family and friends for your favorite cousin's wedding, and just as the bride begins making her way down the aisle your Spidey-sense starts tingling, telling you that danger is in the neighborhood? Or maybe the sun's beginning to peek over the predawn horizon as your head has finally hit the pillow following an all-night henchmen butt-kicking, and you hear screams from the alley below. If you're a hero you can't avoid the need just because you're inconvenienced by it. You can't decline the call or ignore the alarm or hit the snooze—after all, lives hang in the balance. You have to drop what you're doing in order to save the day. So yes, fame, global respect, and literal *abs of steel* are all well and good, but there's not a lot of downtime in return. Given their world is perpetually in peril, superheroes are rarely off the clock, and so every second of their lives is at a premium.

Likewise, we civilian humans are also surrounded by people in need, along with a million different distractions and demands competing for our time and attention, lobbying for our emotional bandwidth, and asking for our outrage—and since we can't do everything, we all have to figure out what we are willing to give ourselves away for. One of the things that happens as you start trying to become the kind of person the world needs is that you realize just how much per capita pain is out there, just how many people are hurting, and just how big a job it is to make it a little better. This often brings a forceful tide of depression, a discouraging feeling that victory is impossible. Rather than being overwhelmed by the scale and ferocity of the malevolence you encounter, your time is far better spent dwelling on what you have to give and where you'll give it.

In the movie *Justice League*, Bruce Wayne is asked what his superpower is; he replies with a wry half smile, "I'm rich." He wasn't just being a Bat-wiseass; he was also speaking truth about being a world-saver: resources are important. Even superheroes need working capital of some kind in order to fight the bad guys, and I'd like you to consider your specific wealth for a moment. We all have three powerful but ultimately finite resources in this life: time, money, and influence, and we begin walking into the life we're meant to have (the kind of life that can repair the planet), by learning how to wisely and responsibly use these resources to alleviate suffering, to generate goodness, to rectify injustice. Our ability to help and give hope is the sum total of these three resources. Generosity is an investment of yourself, in something that is beyond yourself. It will involve giving up a resource that you originally intended to use or hoard—whether you measure that in material things or time or presence or energy or emotional bandwidth. It may be the cash you'd carved out for a new pair of shoes, the rainy afternoon you'd designated for a nap, the weekend hours you'd like to have spent on another Netflix bender, or just a moment to quietly rest uninterrupted. Somewhere along the way to being ordinary heroes we will need to reallocate our resources to become the kind of sacrificial person we need more of, people who are willing to give away something to help someone else.

This spending of resources is the seed of activism of any kind, and it's why generosity and gratitude tend to be kindred spirits. Our ability to be generous is directly proportional to our personal sense of provision; our willingness to give of our time or our finances or our emotional reserve hinges almost entirely on whether or not we feel that we have enough of these things presently. No matter what our bank accounts, careers, or calendars look like, we always view ourselves as living somewhere along the continuum between lack and abundance, between poverty and wealth, between being continually terrified that we will run out or fully confident of our tremendous overflow. And whether we operate out of the former or the latter will dictate how we interact with the world and how amenable we are to giving something good away. It is the difference between holding loosely or tightly to everything that we receive—whether through hard work, luck, or providence. All the really generous people you meet have one thing in common. They operate within a very specific, counterintuitive mathematical understanding: *if I part with something on behalf of someone else, it will be returned to me tenfold.*

My friend David is like this. This algorithm of giving is part of his fundamental operating system. I met David at a church where I served a decade ago, and he and his family were and still are quite superhuman in their apparent ability to multiply themselves, to maximize their waking hours on behalf of other people. They always appeared to have more time than anyone else, despite being as in demand and pressed against their margins as we all are. I'd regularly find them making meals for homeless families, attending student camping events, driving church vans, organizing local work projects, attending church volunteer events, supporting high school athletics—all seemingly at the same time. My understanding of science (rudimentary as it is) tells me that David has the same twenty-four hours each rotation of the earth as I do, that it's not at all possible for him to be in multiple geographic locations simultaneously. I've grown quite sure he's pulling some quantum shenanigans somewhere (or is living proof that the government has finally perfected cloning), because he and his family appear to replicate themselves with astonishing proficiency.

I once asked David about his family's unceasing schedule, and whether his then-teenage daughter and son ever resisted or resented sacrificing so much time and money on behalf of other people. "This is just what we do," he said. "This is our life together, and this is how we live in the world. This is all they've known." To David and people like him, whether motivated by individual faith, altruism, another's struggle, or a matter of conscience, there is no subtraction in giving resources away—there is always an addition. These supergivers know that what they see or learn or allow someone else to experience through their acts of generosity is always more valuable than whatever they parted with. Whether they understand their abundance as fortune or blessings or karma, they believe they're always in the black, always overflowing with goodness, so they hold that goodness loosely and are positioned to share it.

Those of us who aren't as naturally wired for generosity often fall victim to a *when-then* mind-set: *when* we have a little more money, *then* we can start acting philanthropically; *when* we get the kids out of diapers, *then* we'll start working on that nonprofit; *when* we get our shit together, *then* we'll be able to help someone whose has just hit the fan. When we're living life in this headspace of conditional generosity, our start date on a life of radically unselfish altruism is always just off in the distance. We look ahead to a spot somewhere in the future, when we will be secure enough to begin sharing our resources. The problem is that the target we set on giving and helping and doing tends to keep moving—just a few bucks beyond our current bank accounts, just a little more security than we presently have, just a few days beyond this very difficult one that demands our full attention. Greed and self-preservation eventually begin to take over, and we perpetually postpone living more openhandedly because we fool ourselves into believing the timing will one day be better. We imagine some utopian spot just around the corner when everything will be aligned, all obstacles will be removed, and we can finally begin sharing our now sufficiently accumulated wealth. But the world needs the men and women who refuse to wait, those who choose to move without delay. When it comes to lifting people's burdens and being healers and helpers, there *is* someone—it's you. There *is* somewhere—it's here. There *is* a sometime—it's now.

The superheroes who make us cheer on-screen or in real life all reach a point at which they run out of excuses not to answer the call, when the need around them becomes louder and more pressing than the worry about what they will lose responding to that need. When otherwise ordinary people get to that place, they begin measuring their resources differently. They begin dwelling on the inherent worth of the people they're trying to help instead of the perceived value of whatever riches they are giving up—and the choice to help isn't a choice at all anymore. They are *compelled* to give.

Ryan is in the generosity-multiplying business. As cofounder of Culture of Good, an organization looking to connect people wanting to improve the planet in tangible ways, his life is oriented around helping people figure out how to do meaningful work in the world, in showing them how generosity always becomes the catalyst for even more generosity. Culture of Good now engages tens of thousands of employees, customers, and local communities all across the United States through shared acts of generosity, but it all started with one person who noticed a gap in the world and believed he could fill it. Ryan had every reason to shut down and close himself off after losing his mother to suicide when he was only six years old, but instead of letting the experience harden him, he found an acute empathy for other people that moved him to be a giver to the world. Ryan says that "generosity is contagious, like a healthy virus" and he should know. Five years ago Ryan and his wife, Katara, had a dream to give away backpacks filled with school supplies to local children through their small Indiana church. The first September they scraped up enough to buy fifty—and then they kept going, each year momentum for the idea growing, until before long they crossed the thousand-backpack threshold. Ryan then invited Scott Moorehead, CEO of TCC, the largest Verizon retailer, into their generosity movement, and his company jumped on board, ordering sixty thousand backpacks. Over the past five years, Culture of Good has donated backpacks to more than seven hundred thousand children. Ryan has invited thousands of other people into his dream, and he's seen an exponential outbreak of generosity in his community.

Ryan began with little more than a personal quest to help a few kids and a willingness to leverage what he had in order to do it. That's all he needed. When it comes to the riches we have at our disposal, it's easy to suffer from comparison syndrome, to believe our abilities and wherewithal don't measure up. But real catalytic giving isn't something reserved solely for those who hold public office or have amassed a massive Twitter following or influence the culture at large—it is a universal capability. This is what it looks like when we marshal our time, money, and influence to alleviate other people's pain. And this giving gets multiplied exponentially.

My friend Sara Cunningham knows this. She's one of those people who seems to have an invisible wind propelling her life and it, not surprisingly, always tends to carry her into the path of hurting people whom no one else seems to notice or see as worth spending themselves on. As of this writing, she is in the middle of her Free Mom Hugs Tour, a two-week, cross-country journey to ten US cities, where she and other local volunteers she's recruited attend LGBTQ pride events and offer tangible affirmation through warm embraces. (Yes, hugging is a legitimate superpower, and Sara is as gifted as they come.) Knowing how many members of this community regularly face rejection, physical separation, or emotional distance from their parents and family members, Sara shows up to share her story with those willing to listen, and to lavish effusive affection on people who may rarely receive it. It's both startlingly simple and profoundly transformative: give people clear, welcoming *presence* and see how it changes them and inspires others. This is one of the truest revelations about becoming the kind of person who can save the world, and about the generosity required: it is always about matching simplicity with intention, passion with practicality. Mother Teresa said, "Not all of us can do great things, but we can do small things with great love," and Sara is a bear-hugging testament to that simple truth. An embrace is a seemingly small thing—except to a recipient who has been a stranger to it, and to the person who understands this.

Sara's journey to the Free Mom Hugs Tour began years earlier when her son Parker came out, and set her on a path of learning what she didn't know and wrestling with the faith tradition of her childhood. That season in the tempest left her with a fierce mission to be a voice of love and acceptance for the LGBTQ community. Once that internal movement took place, it was simply a matter of deciding what she had to give. Turns out she had *herself*. She had a specific experience and a unique combination of faith, moxie, and mama bear badassery that materialized more and more as she began moving, and yielded a personal activism that doesn't look like anyone else's. No one could or would have responded to this need exactly as Sara had. And no one is capable of giving what *you* can give this hurting world, because your circle of influence, your experience, and your resources are unlike anyone else's. This is why your generosity is necessary and so priceless: because your specific wealth is unprecedented.

David and Ryan and Sara know what all the best comic book heroes know: generosity begets generosity and giving yields giving. When people step into the world to bring their personal resources to bear on the problems around them, they attract other like-hearted humans who want to boost that positive signal. In this way our finite offerings are magnified and we can create something far bigger and more influential than the initial prompt could have ever forecasted. We see this in social media campaigns, in activist movements, in crowdsourcing efforts: generosity snowballs into something far bigger and grander than what the individuals involved could have dreamed of. It's the stuff revolutions are made of. This kind of sacrificial giving is also contagious. Superhumans tend to raise superchildren, to spawn superneighbors, to infect superclassmates, to launch superorganizations, to create superteams.

One of the most beautiful things about sacrifice is the way it assigns value to people. It tells others that they are worth a piece of us, and the affirmation it provides is almost always exponentially greater than the gesture itself. It was certainly the case for me during one memorable encounter in high school. A die-hard Aerosmith fan, I'd planned to see the band over the summer, and as a budding artist I had prepared a drawing of my idol, singer Steven Tyler, certain that fate would smile on me and I'd somehow be able to get it to him. The entire day of the outdoor concert I carted around the cumbersome, carefully wrapped illustration board, fiercely guarding it during the show while pressed on all sides by a sweaty throng of black-shirted teens and middle-aged, balding dudes playing air guitar. As the concert concluded, I led my ten-year-old brother, Brian, through what can only be described as an improvised but highly effective *Mission: Impossible*–style montage of acrobatic fence jumps and frantic sprints around security team members, finally concluding with me brazenly leaping onto the trailer hitch of the band's mobile dressing room. My body slammed hard into the side of the trailer and my face pressed against a window, just a few feet from my microphone-twirling hero. He flashed his distinctive Cheshire cat smile and motioned for me to come to the door at the opposite end of the trailer. When I got there, I nervously handed him the drawing. He put his arm around my shoulder, and told me how beautiful he thought it was. He later asked for my number, and I managed to nervously scribble my name and address on a crumpled piece of notebook paper and hand it to him. I thanked him and then believe I may have levitated home (memories of everything after that being a bit fuzzy).

For a few weeks I was a folk hero in my school: I was the kid who met Steven Tyler. But this newfound celebrity was nothing compared with the nearly legendary status I would attain six months later, when I got home from school and was told by my dad that I'd just missed a phone call—from Aerosmith. I called the number Dad had taken down and reached one of the band's managers. He then told me Steven had written a note that he read out loud to me: "John did a beautiful pencil drawing and I'd love to see if he would send me another one." I'm not sure how to quantify the level to which I felt affirmed that day. The gesture may have seemed rather insignificant to him, and three decades later he probably wouldn't remember doing it—but I never forgot. Every time I hear his voice on the radio I feel the way I did that afternoon. One of my idols told me that his time was worth spending on me. The simple act of his generosity was transformational for me. It validated my talent and inspired me to pursue my passion for art with even more fervor than before. It was a trajectory-changing hope-boost and all it cost was a few moments and a long-distance call.

I don't know you, but I know that you're rich in *something*: time, experience, specific gifts. Whether or not we've had a platinum album, won an election, or graced a magazine cover, we all have the same ability to make people—friends and strangers alike—feel seen, heard, and valued. Openhanded generosity and sacrificial living are how we do this, but these can be a challenge because greed is such a powerful oppositional force. It is in many ways the law of the land. Greed continually convinces us, "I need more than I have. I am in danger of being left without. I can't afford to loosen my grip." The current version of the American Dream tends to be self-based, defining success through accumulation, stockpiling, hoarding, and fending off those who might take what we have. We're taught that keeping what we work hard for is the greatest goal. This is the mind-set of scarcity that politicians exploit to nurture our selfishness, and it's the kind of tribalism that the current president has made a platform pillar out of. Sacrificial givers recognize that humanity is the greater tribe.

The practice of giving doesn't have to be about extravagant gestures or grand displays to do its profoundly beautiful work. The initial investment in other people is usually startling small: set a few dollars aside each month for an organization you believe in; make one call a week to someone you haven't spoken to in a while; give one hour to a local nonprofit or faith community; linger with a stranger for some cheerful small talk; make some bread and drop it off at a neighbor's house. These acts (like all seed investments) will yield far more as they leave your hands and as time unfolds. They will grow exponentially, changing people, who then change other people, and on and on and on—the tidal wave of goodness begins with the tiny ripple of a single act. As you make these seemingly small contributions to the lives of others, you'll begin to realize that what at first felt like sacrifices aren't really sacrifices at all. As you see the multiplying math of generosity at work in your small offerings, you'll soon realize that you're richer than you ever thought possible.

"WE HAVE A HULK!"

—TONY STARK (IRON MAN)

COURAGE

I tend to be increasingly forgetful. It's probably a combination of the overcrowded nature of my schedule, the accelerated velocity of my daily life, or the effects of aging (though I like to blame it solely on the fact that I have young children—a reality which rarely allows me to take a shower uninterrupted, let alone carry any single thought through to its logical conclusion). Whatever the reason, I misplace things a lot, and as a result I spend an inordinate amount of time in lost and found departments of churches, hotels, airports, cruise ships, the occasional shady traveling carnival. There's a specific vulnerability you experience walking up to a complete stranger and saying you've lost something valuable and you hope to God it's there. This humbling confession is immediately followed by the holding of your breath as the man or woman behind the counter opens a drawer, pulls out a box, or steps through some magical door to hidden Lost and Found Land. You're soon immersed in the urgency of that thin, desperate moment, wondering whether you'll get to have a teary-eyed reunion with the treasure you've misplaced—or you'll be sent away in abject despair, where there will be weeping and gnashing of teeth. I confess that more than a few times I've seen items in the lost and found that I'd like *more* than what I actually came looking for, from time to time gazing upon the motley assortment of objects, coveting my neighbor's lost property, and for a split second thinking: "Well, I don't see what I came looking for—but I've always wanted one of *those!*" When we lose something we value we'll often fill that vacancy in any way we can.

By the time we're adults, we've built up a rather large inventory of things we've lost over the years—not just objects and precious material treasures, but other things, too: physical dexterity or mental clarity; people we love and relationships we cherished; the suppleness of our skin; or the ability to sleep through the night without several dazed, pinky toe–stubbing pilgrimages to the bathroom. The accumulation of all that subtraction can begin to crush us if we let it.

My wife and I recently celebrated our twentieth anniversary, and I found myself looking misty-eyed at our wedding albums, shocked at seeing how much younger we looked (okay, how much younger *I* looked), reliving the unbridled joy of the day, and grieving how many people in those images are no longer here. The accumulated losses were startling: my father, my favorite aunt and uncle, our ring bearer, my next-door neighbor during high school, the pastor who married us. The cumulative absence of these people stole my breath and pressed against my heart. It was like seeing myself surrounded by smiling ghosts I once lived with and knew so well. From time to time, I've obviously thought individually about each of those people I'd lost along the way, but seeing that long parade of late family and friends laid out in those pages was an unexpected kick in the stomach on a day otherwise devoted to celebration. Despite all the incredible, gratitude-inducing, life-affirming events and experiences that have come since our wedding, our lives will never be as good as they were when those people were in the world with us. No matter who or what I add to my journey or what victories or successes I have, they will never replace the part that's gone—the void of those loved ones. I guess that's why the word *loss*, while seemingly incomplete, says it all pretty darn well.

Lately I've been mourning the loss of more than just people in old photos—and I know I'm not alone. Ever since the 2016 election, thousands of people have shared their grief over the things they've had taken from them: intimacy with their spouses, connection with family members, lifelong friendships, faith in God, safety in their neighborhoods, trust in their government. These depleting losses steal joy in the present and threaten optimism about the future. For a longer time than we'd have preferred, many of us have been fixated on these losses and able to see little else. However, right now the world needs people who understand that the real story is that there *is* a balance in this living: something born with each thing that dies, something found with each thing lost; there is simultaneously a taking hold, along with each letting go.

Still, the uncertainty and sadness that comes when we lose something precious can be paralyzing. Face enough disappointment and separation, and we can easily start to believe that our losing is inevitable, and worse, that our best days are in the rearview mirror. This can make us terrified about tomorrow, about what other burdens we will have to bear or additional losses we will have to suffer. In turn, we can begin to doubt our own ability to deal with trials and obstacles, which makes them all the more imposing.

As we talked about in Chapter 3, as far as Kryptonite goes, fear is one of the most prevalent and debilitating varieties. None of us are immune to its side effects, no matter how much we try to fortify ourselves or how brave a face we fake. Our politics, our religion, the color of our skin, or the amount of zeros in our paychecks—not one of these things fully insulates us from terror from time to time. And the positively gut-punching, ass-kicking thing about fear is the way it matures along with us, how our nightmares grow up as we do. Yes, our childhoods may have been plagued with snakes and spiders and ghoulish monsters beneath the bed— things that now seem largely ridiculous to our adult selves (though at forty-eight, I'll admit that circus clowns still merit a concerned and lingering side-eye)—but we don't discard fear as a traveling companion as we get older; we just trade in the terrors for more age-appropriate models. Sure, we may leave behind creepy baby dolls and shadowed bogeymen in closets, but we pick up the threats of financial disaster, relational collapse, dying alone, world war, and worrisome spots on CAT scans. As a result, at every age we are equally susceptible to a paucity of courage and a wealth of fear. The Indigo Girls have a song that's been in heavy rotation in my life for decades called "Kid Fears," which asks the questions: "Are you on fire, from the years? What would you give for your kid fears?" I imagine you understand the longing for smaller, older terrors depicted in those lines, that you've looked back with nostalgia on what once seemed threatening. Every one of us daydreams about returning to our previous nightmares, which would surely appear smaller—not unlike our elementary school desks and old bedrooms. The world is full of grown-ups continually pining for the days when their biggest concerns were imagined hordes of zombies, hockey mask–wearing maniacs terrorizing on-screen summer camps, and knowing when to lean in for that first kiss. Maybe we need to realize that the things we're afraid of in this present moment aren't really any more formidable than that. Maybe one day we'll look back and see they were smaller than they now appear. Maybe that's just our darkness playing tricks on us, and if we can shine light into those black places, we can diminish our demons and watch the fear flee.

I can't tell you how many times over the past twenty years I've sat across from desperate, overwrought human beings pushed to the point of breaking, and I've realized that their greatest threat was the fictional story they'd written for themselves (or had written for them by someone else) and accepted as truth. The enemy most assailing their minds in that moment often wasn't the objective reality of their circumstances (as terrible as that might have been) or the hard facts in front of them (as discouraging as they could have been), as much as it was the false narrative they'd inherited via the wounds and the words of people earlier in the journey. As people laid bare their souls to me, their fear usually wasn't just about the real monster in front of them, but the imagined ones they carried into the room. Most of us have a myth we've memorized about our own fraudulence and ineptitude, about our failure and inability to be or do enough—and if we hear that fake news long enough it eventually becomes gospel. We stop seeing the fear at actual size, and like a shadow puppet it gets magnified to appear exponentially larger than it is. Once that happens, once we believe in a distorted version of the truth—all the counseling, prayer, yoga, retail therapy, positive thoughts, primal screams, and personal pep talks in the world can fail to lift us out. Better to avoid the dark places altogether if we can.

For most of us, fear is inextricably tied to control. This is why losing things can be so traumatic, because we feel at the mercy of time, circumstance, or another human being, and this helplessness is often panic inducing. Usually the less about a situation we can maneuver or engineer, the more terrifying it becomes. A few years ago, I decided that instead of trying to escape that fear, I'd climb a high ladder and belly flop into it. I was a pastor at a Charlotte megachurch, and we were sitting down with our student ministry staff to plan that year's youth mission trip. Such short-term, service-based outings aren't remarkable in the church world, and we'd, in fact, crafted a couple dozen by that time, but this was to be a wildly different animal altogether. We decided that this would be a destination-less voyage; we would leave on a designated day without any knowledge as to where we were headed. (Talk about something that sounded easier in my mind.) The trip was conceived as a four-day spontaneous, meandering journey to love and care for people as we met them, wherever we met them, doing whatever they needed. A group of forty audacious teenagers and foolhardy adults signed up for the challenge of tangibly trying to be the kind of people the world needed.

One July morning, after a few weeks of preparation, we spun a Twister wheel we'd converted into an oversize compass, let it choose our direction, and hopped into vans loaded up with tools, camping gear, and care packages. We set out to be a source of goodness in the world, not knowing where it would all lead. (This was a particular challenge to the parents of the dozens of teenagers, who wouldn't be sure at any given moment exactly where their children were or what they were doing.) As we pulled out of the church parking lot I played the part of uber-confident youth pastor, but inside I was a quivering, gassy mess, testing the strength of my resolve and the effectiveness of my antiperspirant. The reality of everything that could possibly go wrong, of all the potential disasters waiting, of my likely termination all flashed before my eyes, and I seriously considered calling everything off before we'd gone a few hundred yards. That was fear trying (as it always does) to make me believe a lie about the future and to sell me on the dire forecast of a week that hadn't even happened yet. (Fear is great at convincing us that the worst-case scenario is, in fact, a foregone conclusion.) Fortunately, something made me refuse to listen to its hissing discouragement that morning, and on we went. Over those ninety-six hours we ended up crossing paths with thousands of strangers over the hundreds of miles we traversed—stopping to help people on the side of the road, performing random acts of kindness in grocery store parking lots and hospitals, sharing meals with strangers, doing odd jobs in homes, and letting one relationship organically lead us to the next. Beyond the desire to help people and give hope, we had no timetable and no agenda. Our only goal was to be available in the moment, to keep our eyes open, and to be moved to move. It was one of the most terrifying and exhilarating weeks of my tenure as a pastor—and my life for that matter.

I'll never forget the thousands of stories we stepped into and the heroic superhumans we met that week. One of them was a woman named Kathy, who liked to be called Kat. Kat was in her late forties and had struggled for most of her life with extreme germophobia and agoraphobia. Living as a recluse much of the time, she carried the weight of her own frightful mental demons, along with the emotional trauma of an incredibly difficult life, like an overstuffed backpack. She sometimes attended the small, rural North Carolina church where we were overnight guests that particular weekend. Kat didn't always show up on Sundays for services, but this Sunday she did. Lauren, one of our high school students, ended up greeting Kat and making a connection with her that defied logic yet needed no explanation. They clicked immediately, finding in each other safety and belonging and something of resonance in the other's story. Without us knowing, Lauren and Kat were being the person the other needed. Kat would normally stand alone in the very back of the church near the doors viewing the service from a safe distance, feeling the security of being able to leave quickly when feelings of confinement would inevitably set in. Since I was going to be up front that morning as a guest speaker, I was told before the service that Kat would almost certainly stay in the periphery of the room, and that I should not be offended or concerned. This held true for a little while, until midway through the service when I extended the invitation for those gathered to receive communion (a ceremonial meal). Out of the corner of my eye I caught a glimpse of Kat tearfully making her way down the aisle with Lauren right behind her, her hands on Kat's trembling shoulders and tears in her eyes as well. Later I learned that it was the first time in twenty years that Kat had come forward for communion. It was as powerful a moment as I have experienced in or outside a church, because I watched someone push through her fear in real time, with the loving support of a stranger. Earlier in the morning, Kat had shared with Lauren the staggering difficulties of her daily existence and the fear she was perpetually struggling to overcome even to be in that room that day. Kat said to her through desperate sobs, "I am trying! I promise that I am trying so hard!" It was one of the best and simplest sermons I've ever heard, and a reminder I've tried to keep pinned upon my heart as I have continued my journey as a pastor, friend, father, activist—and human being: we're all battling our invisible monsters and doing our very best not to let fear overcome our desire to really live. Everyone is trying really hard, and we should go easy on people.

This is the situation every single day, friends. In this spontaneous, meandering trip that is daily life, we are at any given moment surrounded by throngs of people who, despite what we know about their roads or their pasts or their intentions, are trying as hard as they can to figure it all out and to keep it all together, with varying degrees of success or failure. You and I are living with, working alongside, driving past, and waiting in line with hurting, scared, persistent, heroically courageous people who have seen and endured and survived nightmares we can't imagine, and we should approach each of them with awe and reverence, and with a compassion befitting this truth.

Fear usually manifests itself in two distinct ways: it will make you freeze or make you flee, paralyzing you into inaction or slingshotting you into panic. When terror is having its way with you, you find yourself either unable to move or unable to rest. Kat was experiencing each of these sensations simultaneously, so internally assaulted by fear that her mind could never be fully diverted from defending itself, and as a result she could barely function in a practical way. You might not be in as obvious a state of acute trauma as Kat (though you might well be), but you're likely stuck someplace, unsure how to go forward fixing a relationship or rebuilding a career or launching a dream, or completely exhausted from never feeling able to stop and breathe. Whether you're paralyzed with indecision or overwhelmed with anxiety, neither of these is a place you want to stay for very long. Your time here is too short to waste letting your fears, both real and imagined, get the best of you. No, the *best of you* is meant for far more than that. It's meant to radiate brilliant light that chases away the darkness surrounding people.

In one of my favorite scenes from *The Avengers*, Tony Stark (Iron Man) is verbally jousting with the film's antagonist, Loki (adopted brother of the God of Thunder, Thor). As Tony tries to convince Loki that victory is impossible, despite the proceedings up until that point, he lays out the résumé of the recently assembled squad, which seems to do little to shake his adversary's confidence, and after one too many volleys, Tony explodes.

LOKI: *I have an army—*

TONY STARK: *We have a Hulk!*

Tony punctuates the debate by telling his enemy what he's prepared to bring to the fight, and he promises it will be more than enough. I wonder if we can summon this response when faced with things that terrify us, to believe that we are made of something stronger. Fear wants us to believe that we are outnumbered, alone, defenseless—that our demise is secured. When we're in the middle of the fight, its greatest tactic is to obscure what is on the other side of the decision to push back: at best, victory and at worst, growth.

Superhuman courage isn't just about wielding a stone hammer or destroying planet-sucking portals or beating down an army of aliens. It's about getting up in the morning and facing the real shit that scares you: a teenager you can't quite connect with, a spouse who feels like a stranger, a diagnosis that brought you to your knees, a failing business, a piece of predatory legislation that robbed you of sleep—and choosing to move toward it all. The world needs people willing to give fear the finger, because they inspire others to be audacious and brave, too. This is how movements of hope are started: when one or two or fifty people decide that terrible things won't overwhelm them, when people are courageous enough to run into the fray and fight for goodness—even if it scares the hell out of them. When ordinary people remember how strong and brave they can be, the tide turns.

"WHY SO SERIOUS?"

—THE JOKER

HUMOR

I come from a long line of wiseasses. My father was a wiseass, and his father before him, as was his father, or so the legend goes. The W-A gene has been a dominant one in the Pavlovitz family for many generations. I, perhaps more than most in my illustrious tribe, have been prone to bouts of excessive wisecrackery, unchecked tomfoolery, and outbreaks of silliness bordering on sheer folly. Apparently it didn't take long for me to present symptoms either. A few years ago while going through some boxes during my mom's downsizing in the wake of my father's passing, I came across my third grade report card. It was a relic of my budding propensity toward going for the laugh. I'd earned A's across the board that quarter, but in the comments section at the bottom of the yellow card stock, the placid Franciscan nun who taught our class remarked: *John is a smart young man and he is good-hearted, though he tends to be a distraction to the other students by being silly.*

At that tender age there was already a method to my merriment. Certainly humor had a number of practical applications for a young boy trying to navigate the complex minefield of elementary school: de-escalating tense standoffs with bullies, helping make friends in a new crowd, and currying the ever-coveted attention of the fairer sex in which I'd suddenly and mysteriously grown more interested. But the really beautiful thing I learned very early on was the medicinal value of laughter, how it disarmed people when they were uneasy, the way it comforted them in times of grief, the healing work it did in hearts that nothing else could do. Laughter is as powerful and subversive a force as there is on the planet, and yet it's rarely given its due. Most people don't fully appreciate humor, thinking of it as only a frivolous diversion or a defense mechanism—that we "laugh to avoid crying." But we vocational wiseasses know better. We know that a sense of humor is a strategic weapon against sorrow, as effective a tool in battle as anything a supervillain could dream up.

When it comes to disposition, superheroes can be roughly divided into two distinct groups: the brooders and the clowns. Batman is a brooder. Wolverine is a brooder. Lately Superman is as well, tragically. The brooders go about their world-saving with a perpetual scowl, their heavy brows permanently furrowed, their demeanors completely humorless, their hearts nearly impervious to joy. Any smiles come reluctantly. They've experienced tragedy, and this tragedy is something they wear on their faces and carry in their countenance; time and suffering have hardened them. This happens to the best of us, too, at times, as we face the thundering, steaming shit storms of life, and we can't summon the energy for joking or laughter any longer. Over the last couple years, a good number of people have shared that the state of affairs in the world has left them with a heaviness they can't seem to shake, an oppressive seriousness brought on by a steady stream of bad news and a continual parade of worst-case scenarios. Right now laughter almost feels like a privilege, a luxury that only those of us shielded from the greatest harm can afford—but I don't think that's true. I think the more vulnerable we are to threat, the more critical it is to guard our funny bones. As people seem to become more cruel and mean-spirited, our ability to hold on to our lightness makes us bulletproof.

I've always aspired to the Marvel school of slightly subversive heroes, whether it's Deadpool's irreverent fourth wall commentary, Iron Man Tony Stark's staccato running play-by-play, Spider-Man's clever midair quips, or the Avengers' competitive, pinballing banter. I feel at home with counterintuitive humor in the face of profoundly unfunny circumstances. These heroes aren't impervious to difficulty. They haven't been shielded from hell. They have weathered disaster and felt the great responsibility that comes with great power—but they haven't lost the kid inside yet. The dark moments haven't managed to extinguish the light in their eyes. This is one of the greatest assets ordinary superheroes have when despair seems plentiful and hope scarce: they refuse to let the weight of the moment crush the laughter inside them.

The terrorist attacks on September 11, 2001, turned America up-side down in a matter of minutes. Everything from air travel, to professional sports schedules, to television programming was interrupted as the nation paused in shock, and then fear—and ultimately in grief. In the disorienting weeks that followed, a sense of normalcy was almost impossible to come by.

On Saturday, September 29, 2001, while the nation was still freshly mourning and trying to figure out what *normal* looked like moving forward, *Saturday Night Live* broadcast its first live episode since the attacks. The show that evening began with then-mayor Rudy Giuliani flanked by dozens of first responders from the NYC area, many of whom were grieving for their colleagues. After Giuliani made a brief statement on the solidarity and resolve of our nation, SNL creator Lorne Michaels stepped in and asked the mayor a scripted but all too real question: "Can we be funny?" Giuliani responded with a stiff but valiant, "Why start now?" What followed was a big exhale by millions of Americans, who'd been holding their collective breath for weeks, waiting for permission to laugh again. Given that permission we did laugh, though as much in defiance as anything else. As the show tentatively, awkwardly began, my eyes welled with tears and my throat tightened. You could see the strain on the cast's faces, the paradoxical absurdity of trying to mine humor and generate laughter and nail punch lines, even as Ground Zero was still smoldering just a few miles away. I remember thinking to myself, "These people are freakin' superheroes." No, they weren't running into burning buildings or risking physical harm or resuscitating bodies, but they *were* doing something heroic in its own right: they were helping America breathe and smile again, lifting a bit of the invisible but very real weight of the grief the nation had been carrying around on its shoulders. They were helping people recover the lightness that a good belly laugh invites. That night was a statement of defiant resolve to the bad guys, a strident middle finger reminding the terrorists that they'd lost, and a declaration to ourselves that we were going to make it.

Laughter, it turns out, is dangerous, catalytic, and fully offensive in the daily battle to retain hope. Some days the satirists, the comedians, and the jokesters reframe the dire news in a way that allows us to poke fun at it all. This is the humorist's specific gift. The absurdity becomes fodder for a joke that we get to take ownership of and that gives us power to persevere. We can look at a national tragedy, political crisis, or personal struggle and admit that, yes, things are horrible, and yes, to some degree we do laugh to avoid crying, but we also laugh because it affirms that we are stronger than whatever we dare to laugh at. As a pastor and writer and aspiring superhuman, my job is to be alert for people in distress, to listen closely to them, and to try to put into words what they may not have words for. This means sitting with their pain, feeling the depth of their sorrow, and clearly seeing the cruelty of the world that burdens them. The heaviness that comes with this can swallow me up, too, if I'm not careful. On many days when the world seems to have lost its mind, laughter is a lifeline to sanity; it keeps me buoyant and prevents me from sinking into the despair.

One of the people who regularly rescues me with levity is John Fugelsang. He's an actor, comedian, and nationally syndicated talk show host and a fierce and adept laughter warrior, valiantly fighting on the front lines of politics and faith, on behalf of the rest of us who may not be as comedically endowed. His SiriusXM radio show *Tell Me Everything* is a virtual table around which a disparate group of people gather daily to be encouraged, challenged, informed—and invariably moved to belly laughs and spit takes. John's gift (common to all truly great humorists) is his ability to specifically name the ridiculous lurking in the world, and to let us all in on the joke so that we aren't swallowed up *by* that ridiculousness. For so many people (myself included), he is a regular source of respite from the hovering dystopian storms. I laugh along with my friend and feel a bit lighter than I did before—and a bit of my hope returns. Humor tends to do this for us; it softens the blows of injustice, and it makes the despair bearable. It can also effect social and political change in ways nothing else can.

"Humor has always been one of the most effective weapons against authoritarianism," John says. "Generally we laugh at something because we recognize a truth in what has been said and sometimes you get a lot farther with the truth and a good joke than you can with only the truth."

This is the subversive power of laughter; it is cleverly disguised outrage, brilliantly crafted critique, and one of the most powerful forms of activism, allowing us proximity to our adversaries and perspective on our pain so that we can disarm them both. Fugelsang talks about humor's historical precedent and rightly reminds us that it has always been this way. "In medieval Europe, the court jester was the only one who could openly criticize the king, and he could only get away with it because he made it entertaining. People trust good comedians more than politicians or journalists," he says, "because the comedian's agenda is clear—getting a laugh. There's a reason why at the end of the play, the only man King Lear trusts is the fool."

While laughter is certainly a weapon against despair, it's also one that we can easily misuse, as a way of injuring people. My friend has wise words when it comes to the potential violence hiding in humor. He tells me, "As I've gotten older it's become more important than ever to focus on punching up. I try not to mock ordinary people, just those in power." He goes on. "That said, mocking meanness at all levels of society is comedically solid. Attacking ideas is always stronger than attacking people. But sometimes a president makes both rather easy."

Like John, Brian Mayer is another dear friend who I turn to for laughter. He's also a stellar rabbi and a bit of a celebrity at that, having presided over James Franco's bar mitzvah and co-officiated Corey Feldman's wedding alongside MC Hammer. (Yes, you read that correctly.) I met Brian a couple years ago through social media circles and instantly found in him a kindred spirit due to his deep and abiding faith, his fierce heart for equality, and his surgically precise wit. He's gifted with an infectious joy, a buoyant spirit that has a way of somehow making people laugh when they feel more like crying or screaming or throwing up (which is useful in ministry, as the three happen with surprising regularity). We don't get to speak nearly as often as I'd like, but Brian regularly texts me a steady array of silly memes, irreverent jokes, and cheeky observations, which always come as welcome intrusions of levity in increasingly heavy times—unexpected splashes of cool water in the scorching heat of the day. When I asked Brian how he understands humor he said, "The shortest definition is 'perspective.' Perspective turns the horrible story into a funny one—sometimes as it happens, and if not, then in the eulogy as we look back."

One Saturday morning, just a short time after the 2016 election, Brian texted me a photo that was anything but funny. It was the driveway of his Portland home, which had been defaced the night before with anti-Semitic slurs. I immediately called him, and understandably, the shock and fear in his voice were palpable as he recounted his morning and we processed the incomprehensibility of the moment. I wasn't sure quite what to say or how to say it for fear I'd come across as either too dour or too flippant. But the good rabbi instinctively knew how to respond, and it wasn't long before Brian, being Brian, sought to infuse some humor into an otherwise heavy conversation. He quipped, "But at least they left us free chalk!" It took me a second to realize he was making a joke and that it was okay to laugh along. The comment wasn't a dodge, though, by any means. It wasn't pretending something horrible hadn't happened or that it wasn't profoundly troubling. This was Brian seeing things as he always does: through the lens of instructive jocularity. His sense of humor, yielded like Superman's X-ray vision, Spider-Man's web shooters, or Iceman's . . . ice, is a formidable tool in the fight against despair, both his own and others'. I know he isn't trying to escape reality or deny that sickening things exist when he goes for a laugh—he's speaking directly to the sickness, and finding defiant joy to respond with, because he knows that the heart and the funny bone are deeply connected.

My father's death temporarily disabled my wiseass gene. It was really difficult to laugh in the days immediately following his pass-ing. In fact, initially when I caught myself finding something funny, whether on TV or with my children, I stopped abruptly and pivoted internally, the way one quickly changes direction when about to collide with someone on the sidewalk. Humor didn't seem *right* to me at the time, as if my laughter were somehow disrespectful to my father's memory, as if the only appropriate response were perpetual abject anguish. Fortunately the wiseassery soon involun-tarily kicked in and my laughter-fast didn't last long. It would have been a mistake anyway, given that my father had rarely been at a loss for off-the-cuff and often cheeky repartee, or a good bit of well-timed flatulence. In fact, for me and my family in those early days of sorrow, humor quickly became a way to remind ourselves exactly whom we were grieving, how my dad's beautiful foolishness was stored up in our hearts and etched into the laugh lines around our eyes, part of our family's muscle memory. Then, as now, joking was a way of keeping a bit of him alive, resurrecting a part of him here with us.

While preparing for the funeral, my siblings and I huddled around the growing buffet in the kitchen of my parents' home, which is the Italian way. As we drowned our sorrows in copious amounts of gifted pastries and pastas, we began comparing the size of the "grief babies" being formed in our bellies. Soon we were all laughing, and for a few moments the heavy fog of grief cleared, and we could see the sunlight peeking through. I've often said that tears are a tribute—but laughter is no less a memorial to those we love. In fact, holding on to our sense of humor is a worthy fight no matter how difficult the day or troubling the circumstances—if not in the moment, then retrospectively. Enduring the painful conditions outside our windows, on our timelines, and in our hearts becomes nearly impossible if we lose the ability to find humor in this life.

Right now the world needs funny people. It needs people strong enough to reach into the depths of really terrible situations, into days that seem oppressively bleak, and to have the audacity to pull out a rubber chicken and a whoopee cushion. It needs people like John Fugelsang and Rabbi Brian and the *Saturday Night Live* cast and my father, who all understand humor as a weapon against hopelessness, an affirmation that our hearts have remained soft despite how badly they've been injured and how much scar tissue has formed. In days of coldness and enmity, we need good-hearted, compassionate laughter-activists who are able to transform our demons and difficulties into something we can laugh in the face of, something we can mine levity from.

Recently I was talking on the phone to one of my oldest and dearest friends. We were sharing updates on career and family, catching up on each other's lives. I asked him about his parents whom I hadn't seen in years, and he said, "Well, they're doing great—though they've slowed down considerably." When he asked about my family, I in turn replied, "Everyone's doing well. My parents have slowed down considerably, too—especially my father." After a nanosecond of silence we both exploded into laughter, knowing that my father would have fully approved of the audacity of my remark. He would have been thrilled to know I was carrying on his legacy of slightly inappropriate mirth designed to put people at ease in uneasy moments.

It reminded me of a time years ago when I was talking to my father on the phone. He'd had a cancer scare and we were waiting for the results. I was really concerned for his health and feeling bad about being so far away from him. "How are you feeling, Dad?" I asked with what I felt was a seriousness befitting the gravity of the moment. Without pausing for a breath my father replied, "I feel like a shit sandwich without the bread." I laughed. In the middle of wanting to break down and cry, I laughed.

I told you I come from a long line of wiseasses.

"I'M THE ANT-MAN."

—SCOTT LANG (ANT-MAN)

HUMILITY

Ant-Man is a counterintuitive hero in Marvel's Avengers team. Surrounded on all sides by bulging pecs, massive biceps, and freakish displays of brute force, he finds his specific power in his smallness—executing feats at the size of a Skittle that simply couldn't be attempted by the hulking figures around him. Scott Lang, Ant-Man's alter ego, steps into the dizzying bombast of his larger counterparts battling and accomplishes in miniature what enormity never could, and the contrast on-screen is noteworthy.

Watching Scott shrink down to almost nothing and still manage to dismantle exponentially larger adversaries (often from within), we notice something familiar about our own battles. Most of us understand what it is to feel outsized by the trials that come our way, believing ourselves outmatched in the face of disastrous events, toxic people, and terrible circumstances. We *get* feeling like the undersized, under-resourced underdog. It fuels the wars we wage to distinguish ourselves in careers and classes and relationships—always trying to measure up to the competition. In this way, Ant-Man's diminutive stature is inspirational, but it offers another critical lesson for us would-be hope-bringers: there is something transformative about intentionally becoming smaller. In a world of constant boasting, social media posturing, and public horn tooting, there is distinct power in quietly allowing your actions to speak on your behalf, to be okay not advertising your greatness or justifying your worth and to just—be. Humility is at the heart of this personal downsizing, and if you take a quick look on social media or across the cubicle or in the White House, you'll see it is presently one of our true lost arts.

Ernest Hemingway wrote: "There is nothing noble in being superior to your fellow man; true nobility is being superior to your former self." Prince put it another way: "My only competition is, well, me in the past." But most of us aren't content each day to merely go about the quiet work of being a slightly better version of ourselves. We need to one-up the world and then we need to make sure the world knows it and acknowledges it. One day, after I'd posted a bit of subtle social media self-promotion disguised as a casual anecdote, my wife called me out on it. "Nice humble brag!" she said. To which I replied, "Oh, there was nothing *humble* about it, and if it's accurate it ain't braggin'—it's just tellin' the truth!" We both laughed, but she was right—and I wasn't really totally kidding. It's amazing how easy it is to broadcast our achievements and how difficult it can be not to be driven by others' accolades and applause.

In our student ministry in Charlotte we called the idea of intentional, humble living "getting low," taken from a story in the Bible where Jesus bends to wash the filthy feet of his followers in order to show them how to live and how to avoid being steered by ego, vanity, and reputation. Most religious traditions put a high premium on being small, of seeing everyone else as worthy of the same respect. My Christian tradition presents humility as the highest of aspirations, with Jesus extolling the virtues of "taking the lowest place" and caring for others, but these ideas certainly aren't uniquely Christian, or even particularly religious for that matter. Most belief systems and moral codes prize the act of setting aside the ego and moving in a posture of unassuming dignity in service of others. Regardless of your personal faith perspective, you probably recognize the treasure of humility when you experience it in someone else or when you possess it yourself, if only briefly. You know that people who aren't compelled to outwardly enlarge themselves, overestimate their importance, or trumpet their contributions change the temperature of the room; you see the way they disarm people, the ease at which they seem to live. Humble people are rarely unkind—and the rest of us arrogant jerks hate them for it.

Getting low these days is incredibly difficult because we all tend to walk through life artificially inflated, or at the very least feeling like we need to be. Social media magnifies our sense of self, providing us venues to continually showcase ourselves, to livestream our every thought, to package each intimate moment for public consumption and crowdsource approval. Because of this, a subtle but pervasive narcissism guides most of our waking moments. Self-involvement permeates our culture. We can see it in teenagers vying for peer approval, we can sense it in the people we work with, we can watch it scrolling through our timelines, we can read it on a president's Twitter feed: me, me, me. Google reports that 24 billion selfies were uploaded in 2016, which means we really love seeing ourselves—albeit edited, elaborately filtered versions. That Apple decided to fit our ever-present phones with a reverse lens so we could photograph ourselves with ease proved to be one of the most insightful exploitations of our shared desire to be seen and known.

Weaned on a steady diet of reality TV, Snapchat, and Instagram, young people don't aspire as much to be successful or rich or even happy as to be famous. Recognition is now the most sought-after currency, and at an early age people begin to invest their time accordingly. Last week I read the story of a nineteen-year-old man who died after being shot by his wife as part of a viral video attempt gone wrong. He held a book in front of his chest and had her fire a gun at him at close range while cameras rolled, hoping to capture and monetize the moment the book stopped the bullet. It didn't. Instead of an attention-grabbing trick, the young couple captured their disaster and the man's demise for posterity. In so many ways this tragedy was a microcosm of the people we have become: desperate to be seen, clamoring to be known, figuratively (and sometimes literally) dying to go viral. We measure our worth in followers and friends and likes, finding our significance in greater scale and larger bandwidth. On a daily basis, we compete for more market share of notoriety—and we've reached a tipping point of our cultural identity crisis when a reality TV personality known primarily for his boundless, boastful arrogance ascends to America's highest office. This overcrowded world doesn't need more people who are looking to be bigger; it needs people who are trying to shrink a bit, though it's tough to find them, which is, of course, the point.

I often like to joke that I *take great pride in my humility*, but the truth is humble people are difficult to spot because by design and nature they avoid detection and sidestep the limelight. Their transformative work is done largely beneath the radar of our awareness, which is what's so strikingly beautiful and increasingly rare about it. Like the Fantastic Four's Invisible Woman, they are most comfortable doing good without being *seen* doing good, their desire for anonymity part of what drives them and separates them from us attention-starved mortals always striving to be noticed and lauded and praised. For many of us, humility (this purposeful lowness) isn't our first, second, or even thirty-fourth instinct. We've been taught to win and to earn and to achieve—and to make sure everyone knows about it. As hard as it is to be generous or compassionate, when we *do* find ourselves showing kindness or helping someone or being even remotely selfless, the first thing we often want to do is make sure everyone hears about it. Paradoxically, we want to act in quiet humility and yet still feed our needy vanity. I plead guilty of this myself.

A few years ago I was in line at a local quick-serve Mexican restaurant when I noticed a mom from our neighborhood standing with her two sons just behind me. We'd never met, but I knew through mutual friends that she was single and that she'd seen a good deal of adversity since immigrating to America from Croatia a few years earlier. Given the fact that parenting alone for even just a day or so when my wife travels often brings me near tears and causes me to seek out copious amounts of chocolate and wine, I decided to secretly pay for her meals along with mine. After surreptitiously alerting the cashier and getting my food, I quickly retreated to a table across the restaurant and through a planter watched the woman react with giddy disbelief when she learned her meal had been taken care of. Her smile widened and, clearly moved by the gesture, she turned her head quickly, scanning the room to identify its architect. I made sure to stay out of view, and felt a quiet warmth in that moment, simply because of the joy on her face and the knowledge that I'd done something decent for someone who couldn't repay me.

I wish that had been enough. I wish simply knowing that I'd brought some goodness into the life of a stranger had been a fitting reward, but within a few moments I began almost involuntarily carefully composing a social media post to document my good deed, along with a perfectly cropped, well-filtered photo of the scene. "Shit!" I thought to myself, when self-awareness kicked in. I felt sick to my stomach when the unbecoming truth dawned on me: I wanted both to be secretly kind *and* to broadcast my virtue so that others could applaud it. It was equal parts benevolence and self-promotion, and it was embarrassing to realize. I suppose that telling you this story is itself a self-inflating gesture, but I'm rationalizing that I'm doing it as a teachable moment so it doesn't count as a not-so-humble brag. That's one of the commonalities of the superheroes we admire on-screen: they do what they do concealed by masks or hidden in shadow, sometimes to protect themselves, but usually because the helpful act itself is their agenda—not the reward and accolades. The heart of the hero is that as gifted and spectacular as they may be, they see mere mortals as equally important as they are.

Though humility is almost universally treasured, it is usually misunderstood. Many of us have a distorted image of the humble person as some mousy, apologetic nebbish who possesses neither confidence nor courage nor backbone, but this is incorrect. Humility is about balance: it means we neither dismiss nor exaggerate our value. This place of equilibrium allows us to refrain from carrying unwarranted criticism *and* undeserved praise, to not be beholden to public opinion on either side. It is in that elusive sweet spot between self-righteousness and self-loathing that humility resides. When we're in this place, free from feeling like we have to prove our worth or jockey for position, and unencumbered by a pride that needs feeding or an ego that seeks validation, we can simply be present. And like Ant-Man, we do not sacrifice strength for size; our worth is not measured by our stature.

As I said, humble people by definition are often difficult to spot, even when they're close to us. We can easily overlook them in our midst because they aren't seeking the spotlight. I've lived with a humble hero for the past twenty years. My wife, Jen, is a person who naturally lives low. Part of it is her personality; she feels most comfortable out of the spotlight and away from noisy arguments and opinions and tumult. (Unfortunately for her, she's the spouse of an incendiary, public lightning rod.) But it's more than that. Her humility comes from the things she values, from the way her heart works, from her ability to be an advocate for others first, always drawn to the outcasts and oddballs. Jen doesn't lack confidence in her abilities, but she also isn't always looking for outside validation, which allows her to see the need around her and to be more about meeting that need than getting noticed doing so. Being married to a rather emotionally volatile person who exists perpetually in the swirling storm of public view, she's often been the steady, strong, consistent presence in our home—and done so fully in the shadows. This is because she is at home in that smallness that so few people understand. If someone wanted to give her an award for humility, she probably wouldn't accept it.

These days, people like my wife seem like an endangered species. Donald Trump's America has made humility feel like a liability and arrogance an asset—intentionally steamrolling the quiet, unassuming smallness that we're talking about here. His platform and campaign were erected almost entirely on a brash, boastful vanity serving only itself, or appealing to the inherent self-centeredness of others. Getting kudos for "telling it like it is," he made unchecked ego into a worthy aspiration, and millions of people followed suit. As a result, right now the title "ugly American" is an all-too-fitting description of how we're perceived in the world. Our country as represented by the current president and people who share his need to be recognized and applauded is now synonymous with obnoxious hubris. It is marked by shameless self-promotion.

This is why people who are willing to get low are in such demand right now, why there is such urgency for you and me to work at being smaller, because ironically there is a void to be filled by such ordinary superheroes. People's lives are made up of tiny, almost imperceptible hurts and fears, and those tender, cloistered places are inaccessible to those who are too inflated by vanity or bloated by posturing. Like Ant-Man nimbly making his way through the narrow circuitry of a missile streaking toward a crowded street in order to defuse it, humble people can step into the cramped, hidden recesses of people's hearts and disarm them when they are in danger. They can access places that few are even aware of. This is the gift of becoming small: finding that holy ground between not needing to be the most important person in the room and remembering how valuable you are. In that rarefied space, you're able to see and attend to the hurt around you in ways few others can. Seek to rightsize yourself and get low.

"TRUTH IS MY SHIELD."

—DOCTOR STRANGE

HONESTY

I can still remember the first time I ever lied to my parents. I was about six years old. I can recall with perfect clarity the exact spot where I was standing in our Central New York town home when my shameful life of deception began. (Okay, so chances are I'd lied to them well before that, but this was the first time I'd had the self-awareness to realize it.) Strangely I don't recall the actual topic at hand; I only remember my mother asking me a question, me replying—and then immediately sprinting outside and sobbing against a brick wall while a suffocating wave of guilt washed over me as if I'd just committed a homicide. I felt sick to my stomach for the rest of the day, lamenting the horrible thing I'd done, the trust I'd betrayed, and certain I was a hopelessly damned soul for the offense.

But something funny happened: I ended up lying again not long after that, and though an initial internal alarm still sounded, it wasn't nearly as thunderous and didn't reverberate for as long. My resulting queasiness, though still present, was far less severe than it had been the time before. And this pattern continued in the ensuing months: an untruth, followed by an ever-lessening sense of anxiety about it. Soon I began to realize two things: one—lying started not to bother me much at all, and two—I was good at it and rapidly improving! No, I didn't suddenly turn to a life of crime, leveraging such burgeoning talents to engineer global domination, but I became aware (as we all do) of the skill of misleading someone and how effective it was in getting me what I wanted. It's easy to leverage the ability to successfully twist reality and to look convincing while doing it; especially if you happen to be a naturally persuasive person, staying committed to truth-telling is imperative because you are uniquely capable of manipulating people and editing the truth. The first lie is always the most difficult to live with. Each time it gets easier.

I don't know you, but I probably know something about you just the same: you fiercely value the truth, and you prize authenticity in those close to you more than almost anything. You surround yourself with people of unshakable integrity and weed out men and women who've proven prone to deception in the past—or at least I hope so. This is a promising sign that your sanity is relatively secure. There isn't a rational person walking the planet who'd say that he or she wants dishonest people around or that they're intentionally looking to align himself or herself or do business or build a family with con artists and liars.

I myself fiercely *love* truth-tellers, those who don't conceal parts of their lives, beliefs, or motives from me. Whether in my friendships, my business partnerships, my family, my church, or my social network, I like people to come *as advertised* and without a heavily doctored version of themselves where I have to carefully mine for truth in every exchange. However, as much as I like to say that I crave honest people in my life, this is more accurately a half-truth, as I make one notable exception: though I *do* fiercely covet people speaking truth to me about *themselves*, I'm not quite as enthusiastic when they start dispensing such pure, undiluted honesty about *me*. That tends to really get on my nerves. As much as I value full disclosure in others regarding *their* flaws and failings and buried neuroses, I'm not nearly as eager to hear when they believe I'm being hurtful, when my motives seem suspect, when I appear to be yielding hypocrisy. In those moments, truth becomes a much less valuable commodity, and I'm much happier to be in the company of sycophantic yes-men and -women, sweet-talking liars—or at the very least, amenable people who will keep their mouths shut in order to remain ingratiated to me.

We all deeply treasure honest people in theory, but truth-tellers aimed in our direction often don't last very long, or they learn to read the room and to bend that truth in our favor if they want to stay around. It's the reason so many celebrities, professional athletes, and CEOs slip into self-destructive and otherwise unthinkable delusion: they have gradually banished reality and created for themselves a fictional universe where their inner voice is the law of the land and their will is fully insulated from opposition. Nearly every egomaniacal comic book villain is a product of this selective reality making, surrounding himself with perpetually obedient minions and loyal-to-a-fault henchmen. We see their absurdity on-screen from a mile away, but in the trenches of daily life, it can be tough to notice our own ability to create an agreeable narrative.

In the 2016 presidential campaign, then-candidate Donald Trump dropped the phrase *fake news* into the national lexicon to tremendous (and disastrous) effect. He understood how much people value the truth as an idea, and how much they despise being lied to. Trump knew that if you can cast doubt about another entity (a person, a political party, an organization, a segment of the population), if you can make someone believe they're being misled, they will revolt against the perceived offender and they won't require much, if any, evidence to do so. Their visceral response to the mere suggestion of deception will be so great that it will supersede both clear logic and measurable proof. Ironically, in that state of scalding indignation at the supposed lie being proffered, data, facts, and objective reality will be largely irrelevant in convincing them otherwise, because they'll inevitably contend that those arguments, too, could be fake. And down the rabbit hole they go.

Throughout the campaign and his myth-laden presidency, Trump's truth-telling rating on PolitiFact.com has continued to hover somewhere between Pants on Fire and Pinocchio. The *Washington Post* reported that the president offered false or misleading statements more than two thousand times in his first year in office. And yet he himself ascended to the Oval Office largely by casting doubt on the veracity of his opponents, pundits, and critics.

By painting the media at large (which was previously regarded as an authority on establishing fact and fiction for voters) as untruthful, and his political adversaries as all compulsive liars, he was able to dismiss any unfavorable words and to convince a good portion of the electorate that he alone would "tell it like it is." Leveraging people's aversion to deception and the resulting paranoia the suggestion breeds, he made some people feel he was the only one they could trust. Once convinced of that, the toxicity of his delivery and the incredibility of his claims were simply accepted by his duped supporters as the hallmarks of being a straight shooter.

This isn't difficult to understand, is it? If we do even a little bit of introspection, it's easy to identify with people who are willing to be misled in order to hear what they want to hear. It's the reason we ask our spouses if we look good in an outfit we're unsure of, or ask our coworkers to validate a questionable decision we've made, or fish for compliments from friends. In those moments we're not usually looking for truth—we're looking for someone to tell us we're beautiful and wise and totally justified in something we suspect was really stupid. Yes, we all value honesty on its face, but it turns out we're all fairly vulnerable to selective truth when it preys upon our fears, strokes our egos, and confirms our biases. We are all susceptible to believing a more favorable version of the story and defending that story to the death, regardless of the evidence to the contrary.

The world we live in now is one where the truth has become fluid, where the people who best package the narrative, practically speaking, often determine what is real and what is false in order to exert their influence. It becomes possible to undermine authority, research, objectivity, and rationality. And that is a very dangerous game. The antidote—more critical than ever—is for all of us to speak and demand rock-solid truth, even when it hurts or runs counter to what we *want* to believe. Given our collective resistance to telling the truth, it would be nice if we could just force one another to be honest. As a matter of fact, it would be wonderful.

I've always loved Wonder Woman's golden lariat as a beautifully poetic and rightly amusing image—it's an Amazonian lie detector on steroids. There's something strangely satisfying about watching a devious person held in its grasp, revealing every dark part of himself, willing to open up a closet full of bones and confessing his misdeeds to her, thereby ensuring his demise. We get to watch the bad guy selling himself out, simultaneously compelled to tell his darkest truth, while hating himself as he does. Such a tool would be invaluable during presidential campaigns and Senate hearings— not to mention pivotal conversations with a spouse, coworker, auto mechanic, or convincing middle schooler. Sadly though, forcing people to tell the truth with a magic lasso given by the gods isn't an option. In the absence of such persuasive weapons, we have to try as best we can to share life with honest people, and to *be* such people for those we share life with, who (like us) are exhausted from trying to ferret out what's real and what's a mirage in the news, at their jobs, on their social media profiles, across the dinner table, and in White House press briefings. If you've ever been in a relationship with a habitual liar, you know how taxing it is to keep your guard up, to always feel you need to dig beneath the surface, to forever be testing the integrity of what is presented as real. A guy I used to work with was prone to prefacing statements in team meetings with the phrase, "I'm gonna be honest with you." I used to laugh and ask with feigned incredulity, "Have you been lying up to this point?"

Before I began writing this book, I asked my readers what traits they most valued in others, what qualities they wished they saw more of in the world. Honesty was the most popular answer by a large margin, which is telling. It doesn't just mean that it's a coveted commodity (which isn't surprising); it probably means it's one of the virtues people feel is in shortest supply in their everyday experience. In times of drought, the parched ground craves water, and in days when truth and those who tell it are hard to come by, honesty becomes as valuable as pure gold. Trustworthy people are a gift to the world, because they give others a place to rest from the frantic attempt to avoid deceit. The people who tell us the truth without fail allow us to fully breathe in their presence. That's why Wonder Woman's captors always seem oddly relieved when they no longer need to expend so much energy bolstering a lie. Once they reveal the hidden and constantly protected falsehoods, they, too, find rest.

You and I may not have Wonder Woman's lasso or be able to induce the truth from people, but we still need to be relentlessly committed both to being honest *and* to holding others accountable. As difficult as it can be to locate the objective, fixed, unvarnished truth, it is still worth aspiring to. In our romantic relationships, business dealings, and friendships, honesty is how we build up a solid equity of trust with people. Over time, our word becomes a body of work, and people measure us by the veracity of what we've said to them in a million small consistencies all woven together. Every weatherproof marriage, each solid business partnership, every unbreakable family bond or thicker-than-blood friendship is the sum total of all the times someone close to us proved truthful, and how such reliability made us feel. People whose lives are marked by a steadfast pursuit of authenticity are more valuable than they've ever been. And that's the double-portion of this superpower: we get to be honest about other people and about ourselves. We get to be caretakers of the truth in a time when it is scarce and extremely vulnerable—and in doing so we can save the world. That isn't fake news.

ELEVEN

"ONLY LOVE CAN TRULY SAVE THE WORLD."

—WONDER WOMAN

KINDNESS

Sometimes I can be a real jerk: selfish, petty, arrogant, sarcastic, and downright mean—and that's on my *good* days, days when I get the last cookie in the pantry, hit all the green lights heading to the store, and see the cashier waving me into a just-opened checkout line before the surrounding multitude notices and outmaneuvers me. The older I've gotten, the more adept I've become at dispensing bitterness upon the humanity that crosses my path, whether online or in traffic or in my living room. I've often referred to this as the spiritual gift of agitation, and although I should (and usually do) internally despise my profound jerkiness when I become aware of it, far too often I find myself outwardly defending it, justifying it—even celebrating when others applaud it on social media, where the temptation is greatest. Immediately following a successful burn levied on a relative stranger, my conscience's initial protests and my better judgment get drowned out by the intoxicating roar of the crowd, which my needy ego voraciously laps up.

Today our lives are almost exclusively lived for public consumption, with everything on display (our feelings, families, marriages, struggles), and this inside-out living has some disastrous side effects, one of which is that we're more likely than ever to be nasty. Social media has hardened us all, transforming us into professional provocateurs, less apologetic for our corrosiveness and more openly defiant in it. It's as if we devolved into reveling in our malice instead of rightly repenting of it. While we once viewed enmity as cause for personal devastation and something to be avoided at all costs, we now see it as almost a virtue to be flaunted. The more shade we throw, the more addicted we become to the attention it generates, and we find ourselves lowering the bar in search of the applause of a distant crowd of relative strangers.

As someone immersed daily in the public discourse over matters of religion and politics, I carry a heavy sadness seeing the cruelty that now seems standard-issue, the sarcasm, snark, and verbal venom we so regularly wield, and I grieve most when I notice it in the mirror—which I confess is far too often. Sure, these strategies to deflect criticism, avoid meaningful dialogue, or sidestep deep reflection often accomplish their intended tasks, but they also easily alienate and wound people. They aren't a source of healing or restoration or connection—in fact, they often stand in the way of such things. Still, we continue to cherish winning an argument over showing compassion or cultivating humility. We'd rather put our opponents on blast than endeavor to understand them. We have become far too comfortable with our own viciousness. When we publicly skewer people or one-up their insults or shame them silent, we feel quite proud of ourselves. We feel morally vindicated in the moment—even if nothing in our conduct does much to improve humanity in the beautiful ways we're talking about here in these pages (and in the ways we say we want). In fact, kindness's Kryptonite is bitterness, and if you're like me, the past year has seen it gaining traction. It can be a daily battle to keep our hearts soft and to treat the world gently—but we desperately need to.

After all, life is heavy. For most of us, on our very best days, even when everything breaks just right, we're still carrying around the near-crushing weight of our relational fractures, financial pressures, marital collapses, physical illnesses, existential crises, and the frustration that despite both the exorbitant price and the seductively convincing promises of our anti-wrinkle creams—the damn wrinkles never seem to go anywhere. Because of these accumulated disappointments and the daily abrasion we feel, there's an irritability that's always close to the surface. It causes us to easily grow impatient in the checkout line, to erupt in expletive-laden tirades in traffic, to tell off complete strangers on Twitter, and to blow up at our spouses and our kids over socks left everywhere but in the damn hamper. We're all increasingly prone to explosion. We're all in need of kindness to defuse us.

Captain America and Wonder Woman may exist in different comic book universes, but they share the same attractive innocence, the purity of heart and earnest desire for goodness. We see the former character emerge from a different time, and the latter from another land, and we watch them struggle to move against the tide in a world where their simple optimism is passé and antiquated. In their efforts to be people of quiet decency, they are fish woefully out of water. We all understand that alienation, because we've experienced it when we've tried to be softer people in harder times, and it left us feeling out of place in our families, classrooms, workplaces, and social gatherings.

Recently we all watched together as meanness and incivility marched right into the White House and set up camp there. From the very first day Donald Trump declared his candidacy, through the airwaves, at his personal appearances, and via a vitriolic Twitter thread on a continual spiral toward a lower rock bottom, he released the kind of torrential, toxic flood of verbal sewage normally reserved for roadside bar brawls and back alley craps games—and made it all go mainstream. The more vile his commentary on women grew, the more vicious his personal attacks on dissenting politicians became, and the more he stoked the smoldering embers of bigotry, the higher his political stock with certain people climbed.

This was a revelatory moment for the nation, one when behavior and language that would previously have disqualified most folks from even coaching a middle school football team became in the eyes of a good portion of its people, not only permissible, but also sufficiently presidential. To nearly a quarter of the population the toxicity actually became a selling point, and this malevolence has continued unabated through Trump's first year as leader of the free world (as when he called NFL players who knelt during the national anthem to raise awareness of police brutality "sons of bitches" who should be fired). Trump regularly fires off incendiary tweets, berates public servants, and speaks with a rudeness most parents wouldn't tolerate from their ninth grader—and all the while his largely white, Christian base endorses it, amens it, and doubles down in defense of it. Trump has lowered the bar of public discourse to subterranean levels, and too many Americans are thrilled to have official permission to be horrible. The president's behavior has been most damaging in the way that it has given a legitimacy to the kind of conduct once deemed unacceptable in civilized society, it's emboldened people to be open about things they used to conceal for the sake of decorum, and it's placed many already oppressed Americans in the path of a river of vitriol that has wildly breached its banks.

I spend a good deal of my days listening to the stories of members of already marginalized communities who feel more and more pushed to the periphery because of the enmity that's been rewarded with the seat of the greatest power on the planet, and has trickled down into our social media exchanges and personal interactions. A few months ago I attended an interfaith meal in Murfreesboro, Tennessee, called A Seat at the Table hosted by my friend Abdou Kattih, who is Muslim. Abdou created the monthly gathering to help people from disparate communities hear one another's stories and to do work together in their city around which they all aligned—which turned out to be in lots of ways. There were thirty of us seated around a huge U-shaped table in the banquet room of a new Indian restaurant, and one by one we began to introduce ourselves and to share whatever we felt compelled to with the group. There was a thread of exhaustion running through all the stories, with many saying that they felt a fatigue and despair of the spirit as a result of the cruelty they've witnessed over the past year. Each person came to that table because in both similar and in extremely specific ways, they have experienced America's new bitterness, and they have grieved the loss of decency that accompanied it. One of the most poignant comments came from a Muslim woman who appeared to be in her early fifties. Her voice had been steady and buoyant as she started to speak, but it began to quiver as she said, "I've lived here all of my life and it always felt like my home—until now, until this year." She and her husband went on to talk about the difficulty of being used as the face for terrorism and becoming the targets for so much misplaced rage.

Bullying and bigotry haven't been this fashionable in decades, confederate flags seem to fly in more windows, racial slurs appear to be scrawled across more front doors, middle fingers fly more quickly, and anti-Semitic epithets seem spoken with greater audacity. In this country on all fronts, we've experienced a Renaissance of Cruelty—and it's time to end this era.

Augustine of Hippo once said, "Hope has two beautiful daughters; their names are Anger and Courage. Anger at the way things are, and Courage to see that they do not remain as they are." If that's true, the first of these two children is certainly far easier for us to deliver than the second. We rarely have to work for anger; it is an almost involuntary response to the dysfunction and injustice we witness as we live and move through our days. That knee-jerk reaction that makes our blood boil, our jaws clench, and our fists ball up doesn't require much more from us than showing up—which is probably why our Twitter feeds, talk shows, and even our heads are so filled with fury. The far more difficult task is to find the courage to do something tangible with that rage, something less violent, less destructive, and more decent than whatever incited the anger to begin with. Such bravery is often a matter of remembering how strong we're capable of being.

The path to a kinder world begins with kinder people—and the way we become those kinds of kind people (as with many of the truest truths of this life) is both startlingly simple and incredibly elusive: we try to live in such a way that we hurt people less. The Latin phrase *primum non nocere* is part of all health-care students' education, serving as one of the unspoken core principles of those who go on to serve as doctors, nurses, and other caregivers. Roughly translated as "First do no harm," it is the promise to protect a patient from undue injury, to do everything in your power toward that goal, and to avoid doing further damage to someone in the process of trying to save a life. I suppose if we were to commandeer and paraphrase these sentiments for the purposes of becoming the kind of people the world needs, and to craft a good rule of thumb regarding the hurting, heartbroken people crossing our paths every day, the pledge might be restated: *Don't be a jerk*. It sounds elementary, and yet it's actually a master's level civility course, and too many people are skipping class and dropping out. So I'll offer my notes here:

> **SPEAK LOVE.** Offer kind words to as many people as you can: strangers, friends, social media acquaintances—and most of all, to the people close to you who you may have forgotten need them. Give compliments and encouragements freely.

SMILE AT PEOPLE. In a world that has grown more acerbic and mean, the people you encounter are likely starving for simple warmth—and you can feed people without needing to say a word.

EXERCISE SIMPLE DECENCY. Hold doors for people, offer to help them with their bags, let someone have the closer parking spot, overtip a server.

ANTICIPATE A NEED AND FILL IT. Keep your eyes open for people around you facing difficulty: a surgery, a layoff, life after losing a spouse, a tough exam schedule—and step into that space by doing something without needing them to ask.

A friend of mine has been known to say, "I know a guy who got straight A's and flunked life," in reference to people who've outwardly had success but done so while forgoing simple acts of kindness and goodness. Chris Ulmer is clearly passing life. You may have seen the video circulating of this special education teacher at Mainspring Academy in Jacksonville, Florida, who begins each school day by looking each child directly in the eye, smiling widely, and paying each of them a specific compliment. In the video, you can see the children's faces change dramatically as they absorb these personalized words of affirmation delivered with clarity and affection. Watching it all, there's no doubt such encouragement is invaluable in the moment, and critical in sustaining each of his students during a typically difficult school year—but there's also little question that Chris's words and gestures will long outlive these children's time in his classroom. His acts of kindness and care will reverberate for decades, becoming a central part of the adults they grow to become, ones whose paths are irrevocably altered because one person decided to tell them what he saw in them that they may not have seen at the time.

The world needs more people like Chris, whose default position is benevolence, who feel burdened to do no harm, who are daily compelled to try to be decent. And as with most of these ordinary superpowers we're seeking to cultivate, this kindness we're bereft of is not found in the bombastic and the noteworthy and the attention-getting, but in the small and simple ways we show people grace well beneath the radar.

Kindness is the antivenom to the cruelty we're saturated with, handling people with care, treating them with a softness that they so rarely encounter these days. Aesop once said, "No act of kindness, no matter how small, is ever wasted." But far too many such acts are avoided altogether because we underestimate their transformative power and don't realize the great urgency of those around us. Many people we cross paths with are hanging by the thinnest of threads. By showing them simple attention, affection, and kindness, without knowing it, we get to strengthen that thread. Go easy on people. Treat them gently. Be the kind of kind people who can save the world.

TWELVE

"IDEAS ARE BULLETPROOF."

—*V FROM* V FOR VENDETTA

CREATIVITY

My friend Dana recently shared on social media that he'd been suffering headaches for a few weeks, that he'd been irritable and had difficulty concentrating. (Such things are regular occurrences for me these days and almost internal white noise, but for him it was unusual and cause for concern.) After talking to his wife about it and taking an inventory of his daily practices and routine, he noted that he hadn't been drinking any water at all. He'd consumed coffee and soda almost exclusively. Wondering if this might be a source of his recent ailments, he began steadily drinking copious amounts of water, and in a day or so he began to feel a hundred times better, and his symptoms gradually subsided. Dana hadn't realized that he'd been chronically dehydrated, which is actually quite common. In the past I've worked as a personal trainer, and one of the things I would always tell clients is that you have to drink water when you're not thirsty. By the time you actually feel thirsty it's too late—you're already dehydrated, and you can't just catch up immediately on hours or even weeks of neglect. You really need to consume the water required for your workout well *before* your workout. Continual hydration is the secret to maintaining physical health.

Recently I have noticed an internal heaviness, an irritability and sadness that worry me. Like my friend Dana, I did an inventory of the daily rhythms of *my* life and I realized: I am spiritually dehydrated; I am emotionally parched, chronically joy-deprived. For months I've been walking around without regularly allowing my soul to be replenished, largely avoiding life-giving activities, waiting for circumstances to feel favorable enough to let lightness return. If you woke up into this day feeling anxious, irritable, and exhausted, there's a good chance you are similarly parched, that you, too, are spiritually dehydrated. Creativity is what rehydrates dry people. Songwriting, painting, cooking, fixing cars, scrapbooking—staying connected to our muses helps us tap into the things we love and are passionate about. We're wired to seek pleasure and spiritual stimulation. So we can't afford to let those creative muscles atrophy, because they sustain and renew us.

In both the Iron Man comics and movies, the titular hero's alter ego, Tony Stark, has a glowing light in the center of his chest that keeps him alive. (For 100 Geek Points, it's called a mini arc reactor, and it prevents the shrapnel that was embedded in Tony's body during a terrorist mortar attack from moving into his heart and killing him instantly.) In a hilarious scene from the first film in the franchise, Tony's erstwhile assistant (and future love interest), Pepper Potts, finds her boss lying quietly on a table in his lab, clearly in acute distress. Pointing to the mass of steel and wires in his hand, she asks, "Is that the thing that's keeping you alive?" To which he replies with typical deadpan understatement, "It *was*." Pepper is then given the critical task of reaching into the oozing cavity in Tony's chest and quickly connecting the hanging wires to a replacement reactor before he expires, all while avoiding letting the wire touch any metal and electrocuting him à la the board game Operation. The scene is both slapstick and touching, reflecting the urgency of the moment and underscoring the intimacy between them. After a few tense seconds, Pepper locks the hardware in place, and Tony's countenance changes as the light in his chest glows. He's fully alive again. I bet you understand Tony's predicament waiting for Pepper's arrival. I imagine you know what it's like to lose the light inside you and to feel yourself low on life and passion. I think you've spent more than a little time somewhere along your journey trying to recapture the spark in you that has begun to dim because of how dark the world appears. You may even be in that dark place of desperate waiting right at the moment, and if so, you're in good company.

Often when our lives or the world looks bleak, we retreat in our despair and lose the desire to create and to play. We abandon the daily pursuits that give life meaning. We stop painting, writing, and cooking; exercising, eating well, and meditating. We divert that otherwise life-giving, hope-inducing, stress-alleviating energy into simply managing grief. This is why the world needs people who create, right now more than ever, because that glowing light in the center of *our* chests and the spectacular art it produces is life-giving, not just to us but to the world. What we make becomes a conduit of joy, traveling to others and then returning to us, multiplied exponentially.

For me, music in particular has been this source of emotional and spiritual lift when I have felt that inner sinking. A few weeks ago I was lying in bed, phone in hand, doing what I'd grown used to doing each morning: scanning the social media horizon and finding more than enough to derail my spirit before I'd even set foot on the ground. As if on cue, my blood pressure started to rise and my hope evaporate. It was going to be another day in Twitter Hell—until I noticed that U2 was playing a show that night in DC, which is a good four-hour drive from NC, if traffic on 95 isn't horrible (and traffic on 95 is never *not* horrible). I didn't have a ticket, I'd have to leave in a matter of hours, and I had a ton of important work I needed to do, but suddenly I needed to do something *more* important: I needed to stand in the middle of a stadium with fifty thousand strangers and sing, "*It's a beautiful day . . .*" I needed to get out of my dry and brittle rut and to cultivate some fresh hope. My spirit quickened, as if sensing a glorious disruption was coming. I mentioned it to my wife, who, having lived with me for twenty years, found such wild impulsiveness perfectly normal. "Sure, go!" she said. I scored a ticket online and was in the car soon after. The traffic on 95 was in fact horrible, but it was an acceptable annoyance. I reached the venue with a few moments to spare, and by the time the sun set on a day that had begun quite ordinarily, I was standing in a pulsating sea of humanity, as the Edge's shimmering chords washed over us, and Bono led us to church with the opening call to prayer:

"The heart is a bloom . . . shoots up through the stony ground." My end-lessly racing pulse finally slowed, the ever-clenched muscles in my jaw released, my labored breathing stretched from short, shallow sips into slow, savoring swells. My chest expanded and contracted fully without interruption, and my mind no longer chased what had been or might be or should be—but paused to quietly rest in what *was.* I drove home at 1:00 a.m., exhausted but nourished. I'd had my sense of optimism recalibrated. Guess that really is the power of three chords and the truth.

Mya Hunter understands the power of story to change peo-ple and to flip the prepared script. She is the executive codirector for SpiritHouse, whose curators describe as "a black women–led cultural organizing tribe in Durham, North Carolina, with a rich legacy of using art, culture, and media to support the empower-ment and transformation of communities most impacted by racism, poverty, gender discrimination, criminalization, and incarcera-tion." Even before finding herself on the front lines of local activ-ism and working as a social justice champion, the arts had been Mya's constant companion. As a young girl, creativity was refuge and sustenance, what she described to me as a "safe place to get lost inside, the place where I could dive into the well of emotions I had without drowning in them." When Mya was sixteen, her family's home (built by her grandfather's hands) was foreclosed on, thrust-ing her into chaos during what is already one of life's most tumul-tuous periods. As she and her family grappled with meeting their urgent and mounting daily needs, Mya realized that no one was coming to save them. She began to understand the systemic nature of poverty, displacement, and incarceration, and just how difficult it was for families around her to extricate themselves when adversity came. Rather than lamenting everything that seemed beyond her control, Mya decided to do what she could. She began volunteering with a local nonprofit, working as an advocate for families just like hers and helping to fix the broken systems so many find themselves in. Mya says that she initially wanted to "help shift the reality for myself and my family," but she's since done that for thousands of families, in a career of community organizing now entering its second decade.

This is why being the kind of person the world needs right now means having a creative vision: seeing what the world *could* be in a way that others may not be able to. Mya's lifetime love of science fiction and fantasy helped her find a language for transformative social justice work by showing people the incredible imagination necessary to create entire worlds that did not exist in the reality in which they were conceived. "We have to be able to imagine a world we've never known," Mya said to me, "while acknowledging the one that has existed." This is essential, she says, so that we don't simply replicate toxic systems of our past. "This takes some radical imagination and a willingness to lean into the unknown."

Friends, this is precisely why the act of creating is so soul-nourishing during days when we are discouraged and depleted, days that steal our muses away. When the present circumstances overwhelm us (as they so easily do), we can imagine, paint, play, and write our way from the world that is and toward the world we *wish* to be. This is not mere escapism; it is intentional time travel, helping us step into the future in ways that are transformational.

Creativity is our conduit and path to this bright future, because it unearths our passions and allows us to make the abstract tangible. Former SpiritHouse board member and movement ancestor Nayo Watkins often said to her community, "You already know all you need to know; it's in your bones." When I asked Mya what kind of person the world needs, she had a simple answer: "The world needs more artists." She added, "The world is full of beauty and stories, and artists help us see it all with fresh eyes; they help us heal from the trauma of our ancestors." It's telling that for Mya, success in the work she and SpiritHouse do together is measured in creativity, too. "Getting my community to imagine a world without prison, without oppression. When folks begin to come to larger tables with that kind of radical imagination, that's a real success to me."

Creativity is one of the greatest weapons against despair and hopelessness because it is so versatile. It changes form depending on the hands that wield it. Creativity can give us a language for grieving and celebrating; it can be a form of activism, an expression of faith, an act of communion with others, an embracing of identity, a reclaiming of story. It can be an agent of change and a balm for those in pain. Creativity is both an outlet and offering of expression, something given and received.

Many religious traditions speak of the soul, that *spark of the divine* inside each of us that transcends our blood and bone, and whether or not you claim faith of any kind, you've probably experienced instances of doing something you love and find joy in, moments when you know you're in the sweet spot of your calling, when you feel connected to the world in a way that transcends description and cannot be quantified with words. Creativity is a portal to our imagination. Albert Einstein said that creativity is "intelligence having fun," a perfect description because it reminds us what an elixir the act of making and building and doing is to our world-weary souls, the way it rouses our intellects and imaginations back to life when we sustain emotional wounds. The act of creating does more than simply generate images, or make music, or start a business—it allows us to give people joy, using the very things that give us joy. As they say, art does imitate life.

For thirty years Bob Ross has been my Yogi, my Jedi master, my Professor Xavier. The afro-donning, velvet-voiced PBS painter first became a fixture in my living room during college afternoons, while I was an illustration major on a scholarship to University of the Arts. I wasn't particularly captivated with Ross's actual artwork per se (as unique as it was). For me and for millions of people like me, it was about a whole lot more than the almost sleight of hand landscapes he assembled in just under twenty-three minutes. There was something else happening in between the happy little trees and big ol' mountains, something almost spiritually medicinal. Bob Ross wasn't just teaching you how to paint—he was sharing intimate space with you, telling stories to you, and affirming your worth with little more than a canvas and a palette as his tools. This was a soul hug dressed up as an instructional video. It was subversive and covert encouragement.

And it wasn't as though Bob Ross's life was as boundlessly cheerful as his landscapes. He'd experienced divorce, the death of his second wife to cancer, and the passing of his mother whom he'd lived with for many years as an adult. If you look and listen carefully, you can find the sadness tucked away in his sunny exchanges with the viewer. Many times in quick asides during his show, he'd describe an old, misshapen tree by saying, "He had a hard life—like me." He dedicated one particular painting to his mother who was in the hospital at the time of the taping. Another time, he talked about the hard times being important so you could appreciate the good times when they came, adding before returning to his easel, "I'm waiting on the good times now." Bob used his creativity as a tool to care for people, knowing how it felt to need care. He leveraged his natural talents to bring comfort because he knew what it was to need comfort. He filled the holes he saw in the world using oil paints, fan brushes, and palette knives. Twenty-two years after his passing, his show still runs in heavy rotation and his popularity endures, and I think it's because people are still calmed and inspired by his presence.

Austin King Hurt lives on the east side of Indianapolis with his mom and four siblings, a lively group that he told me he's happily "stuck right in the middle of." At first glance, Austin is a fairly ordinary eleven-year-old, but he has another not-so-secret identity as the Young Urban Gardener, an elementary school–aged hero who doesn't fight crime, but hunger. Austin's origin story happened when he was just eight years old, watching his mother prepare dinner for the family. It was a simple menu of rice and beans, which, as sometimes happened, didn't seem like enough for everyone in the house. While his mother was out of the kitchen, Austin's mind started dancing and he hatched a plan. He thought to himself, "I could grow beans here in the yard, and then we'd *always* have enough!" With no agricultural experience (other than believing water, soil, and sunshine would be sufficient) he took a bowlful of beans outside, and in a beautiful twist on the story of

Jack and the Beanstalk, he buried them in the yard. A week later, sprouts shot up through the ground. They've always had enough beans since then.

But Austin's mind didn't stop dancing just because *his* family was better off. Knowing so many other families around him were struggling to fill the table, he realized, "If I can feed myself and my family—I can feed everybody!" In addition to starting his own You-Tube channel with gardening tips for both adult and child garden-ers, in May 2017, with the help of a neighbor who donated some of her land, as well as a small army of local volunteers who've ral-lied around him, Austin launched his first community garden. He shared with me his vision for the garden and the invitation he offers the people in his neighborhood: "I grow it and you take it." Austin plans to go to school to study agriculture and to begin raising live-stock; his destiny is to help lots of people. I don't doubt him for a second. With his tender heart and entrepreneurial mind, he'll be unstoppable. Austin's story reminds us that creativity isn't just about having skilled hands or perfect pitch or an eye for composition—it's also about having a vision that no one else can see, about imagining the world that *could be*, and knowing what to do so that it becomes the world that *is*. There is artistry in engineering this transforma-tion.

This life is a creative act. We are made to be makers. We make friends and we make enemies. We make mistakes and make amends. We make memories and make love. We make babies, we make messes, and we make our moment-by-moment marks on this planet in a million different ways, in the thin space between the sun rising and setting each day. We are each a collection of small, continual acts of creation and re-creation. You have been "making" your way right up until this very moment, and you can look back on your story so far and see all you have been cocreator in—relationships and families and faith communities and career partnerships and neighborhoods. You have always been making things, whether you were holding a paintbrush forming happy little trees on television, doing community activism using the arts, or simply trying to nudge your high schooler through another hormone-ravaged day filled with pop quizzes, text breakups, and massive waves of emotion that come without a discernible source. You *need* to be creative to navigate such storms. When I speak about creativity, your thoughts might naturally gravitate toward the obvious, tangible activities that first come to mind, and if such things aren't part of the regular rhythm of your life, you might believe yourself disqualified from the discussion. And yes, that is certainly part of what the world needs. It needs art and music and scrapbooks and birdhouses, because those things all help tether us to sanity when the tempests threaten to rip us from our moorings, but it also needs the quieter, subtler artistry found in rallying people for a cause, organizing political campaigns, mounting protests, and synthesizing the gifts of disparate people.

In difficult days, creativity is more critical than ever so that we do not allow our spirits to grow brittle, so that we can be replenished, so that we can be reminded to live, so that we can be the muses for others who are dry. Do the things that give you joy, that come from the deepest places within you. Follow your muse because that will keep your heart soft. Use your hands and your voice and your body to make the poetry of this life, and do it as often as you can. Stay hydrated out there.

THIRTEEN

"I CAN DO THIS ALL DAY."

—CAPTAIN AMERICA

PERSISTENCE

Every superhero movie worth the ticket price includes a training montage: a rousing, swiftly edited collection of scenes featuring our heroes (alone or alongside their muscle-bound brethren) as they hone their skills, harness their powers, and prepare for whatever fierce adversaries might soon show up to level the city or steal the moon or convert humanity into a zombie army. We love to see our heroes breaking a sweat and putting in the work, and we know that sometime in the future (hopefully in the next forty-five minutes) they will be called upon to dig deep from that well of shed perspiration and plasma to face their coming *destiny moment*. And when this transformational moment *does* arrive for our heroes, we watch them run into the trenches without hesitation. Because we watched them prepare, we'd be crushed if they never got a chance to actually *be* super, if they catapulted themselves into battle, took one good punch, and folded—hanging up their spandex, retreating to their day jobs, and retiring from the hero business altogether. That would be one lackluster blockbuster. None of us wants to watch ninety minutes of Clark Kent at the *Daily Planet* working traffic reports or covering grocery store openings and dog shows when we know he could be spinning the actual planet. We want to see Superman get the snot kicked out of him and be buried beneath a building, and we want him to reach his hand up through the rubble and fight until he prevails.

Before being injected with a superserum that transforms him into the near-perfect human specimen eventually known as Captain America, Steve Rogers is just a skinny, undersized kid whose massive heart is too big for his tiny sunken chest, a regular guy who wants to fight for his country in World War II but isn't built for it—at least physically—and is rejected. In a scene from his eponymous film, Steve's just stood up to a movie theater bully talking loudly over a military tribute film, and he soon finds himself in a nearby alley being thoroughly pummeled by the small mountain of a man. After a series of seemingly jaw-breaking blows sends Rogers repeatedly into the concrete but fails to keep him there, his assailant makes an observation: "You just don't know when to give up, do ya?" The frail, breathless, bloodied, soon-to-be national hero raises both fists in front of him, and in a declaration that seems to be meant for himself as much as the bully, says, "I can do this all day." It's a phrase he will repeat decades later, after being brought back to life in the present day and facing even greater resistance and far higher stakes than simply his honor. But that moment in the alley dozens of years before reminds us that Steve Rogers has the heart of a hero, and he will not be one for quitting just because his lip gets bloodied.

The Philadelphia Eagles have had their share of bloody lips. The team hadn't won a Super Bowl in its eighty-five-season history, and it wasn't going to win one in 2018—at least not after MVP candidate and second-year superstar quarterback Carson Wentz went down late in the season with a catastrophic knee injury. Though they'd already nearly locked a playoff spot and eventually eked out two wins to secure home field advantage throughout the playoffs, the prevailing wisdom from football fans and pundits around the country was that the team didn't stand a chance of going very far with backup QB Nick Foles at the helm.

Apparently nobody told Nick Foles that—or he was too busy busting his butt to pay much attention. After a promising start upon entering the league in 2012 playing for the Eagles, Foles had been inconsistent and was later traded to the Los Angeles Rams. He struggled there as a starter, and by 2015 he was seriously contemplating retirement while on a head-clearing fly-fishing trip with his brother. When he emerged from the literal and figurative wilderness, he received a call from his old coach, Andy Reid, who'd originally drafted Foles in Philly and was now coaching the Kansas City Chiefs, asking him to give it one more shot. He consented, and after a year there, Foles was traded back to the Eagles, where he fully expected not to get much playing time unless disaster struck—and then disaster struck (or at least what seemed like disaster). Over the course of the playoffs, Foles performed beyond anyone's expectations (except for his own, his coaches', and his teammates', who'd been steadfast in their support of their number two).

One day after the Eagles' unthinkable victory in Super Bowl LII over the NFL's reigning champions (and perpetual superpower), the New England Patriots, Foles, who had played brilliantly and received the MVP award, gave a press conference and talked about the road to that spot. "I think the big thing is don't be afraid to fail. In our society today, with Instagram and Twitter, it's a highlight reel. It's all the good things. When you look at it, when you have a rough day, or you think your life isn't as good as that, you're failing. Failure is a part of life. That's a part of building character and growing. Without failure, who would you be? I wouldn't be up here if I hadn't fallen thousands of times, made mistakes. We all are human. We all have weaknesses."

Nick Foles understands that persistence isn't about a moment, it's about a process; it's a skill developed over time and distance, and it's forged in the fire of what appears to be failure. Persevering through struggle is sometimes simply a matter of staying a little bit longer—even when you feel you've given everything you have and it doesn't seem sufficient.

He continued, "When people speak and they share their weaknesses, I'm listening, because I can relate. I'm not perfect. I'm not Superman. We might be in the NFL and we might have just won the Super Bowl, but we still have daily struggles. That's where my faith comes in. That's where my family comes in. I think when you look at a struggle in your life, just know that it's an opportunity for your character to grow."

Nick's story underscores that there is wisdom in the act of staying, because it allows you to let events play out beyond that moment. It allows everything to align in ways you couldn't predict or arrange, and you get to see the fruit of sticking around. As a die-hard Eagles fan, I'm glad Nick Foles stayed. If you're from New England, you probably wish he'd have called it a day.

In this era of simple bankruptcies, quickie divorces, and overnight free agent trades, staying and fighting are lost arts. In businesses and relationships and on professional sports teams, people don't stick around the way they used to, which is why being the kind of person the world needs is sometimes a matter of enduring failure, discomfort, and disappointment long enough so that you're where you need to be when you're most needed. Persisting is about withstanding the difficult days and outlasting the storms and taking on the messiness that others can't or refuse to.

Relationships are places where such messy staying is paramount. Whenever I counsel couples preparing to get married, to their surprise we end up talking very little about what marriage *is* and a lot more about what marriage *isn't*. It isn't a singular, celebratory moment like their approaching wedding day. It isn't the pleasant emotions that tend to be plentiful early on. It isn't a warm feeling of easy affection toward the other (as such feelings are almost involuntary at first). We talk about all this so that they know that their impending promise of "for better or for worse" will likely include a good deal of decidedly *worse*, that "'til death do us part" is a lot longer than it might seem at the beginning. I want these couples to know exactly what they are (and aren't) signing up for so they understand the gravity of the vows they'll be making—and so that they learn how to stay when leaving is easier and less taxing.

Jen and I have been married for twenty years and began dating two years before that, though we first met a year earlier. Early on she didn't care for me all that much. I like to say that it took her twelve months or so to fully comprehend my specific greatness, to realize just how perfect we were for each other, and to grasp how foolish she'd have been to let me slip away. She was not at all convinced of any of these things initially, and she'd have laughed you out of the room had you suggested them at the time. I could (and often do) make all sorts of jokes about slowly wearing her down, and about her accepting my proposal in a moment of weakness or bad judgment, but the truth is, when we met we weren't ready to become what we would become: something strong and enduring.

When our paths first crossed in college, Jen's parents were on the verge of a divorce and the tremors were shaking the bedrock of her life, while I was reeling from a disastrous relationship implosion and tiptoeing into an adulthood that I wasn't quite enthralled with. We weren't at our best when we met, and we certainly weren't ready to be caretakers of another human being's heart. Our *destiny moment* hadn't arrived yet. She needed time to sort through grieving the loss of the family she knew, and I had to heal and get my sea legs underneath me in order to be steady enough for her to lean on 'til death do us part. We weren't aware of it then, but that year was about each of us waiting for the kind of magical alignment that lasting relationships, business ventures, career turning points, and personal growth moments require. Sometimes persistence is about doing the daily work long enough to let people, circumstances, and the world catch up with you. Sometimes you need to realize that you're holding on for more than just yourself.

In *Spider-Man 2*, Peter Parker, struggling to get his wall-crawling groove back, attempts to leap to an adjacent rooftop, and after a brief moment of airborne jubilation, ends up falling precipitously through a clothesline filled with hanging underwear and careening off two parked cars before slamming hard into the pavement. It's a tough and quite literal coming-down-to-earth moment—and yet he doesn't stay there. He doesn't allow that fall to be the final act in his story (much to the relief of those whom he'll later save from calamity). This is why it's important to press through our disappointments, to endure the bruises to our egos, to withstand the embarrassment that comes with failure: because on the other side of all that hell, people will be helped. There are human beings whose names and faces you may not even know, but whose futures will be changed by you persevering in whatever you're presently struggling with. It's one of the most profound and humbling experiences of life, the effect we can have on someone, or how a chance connection or meeting can make all the difference in helping someone persevere.

I met Brandon three years ago. He was then a high school senior from the suburbs of Chicago, who'd reached out to tell me that this life had grown too painful to endure, that he was exhausted, that he wanted to leave. Later that night I began corresponding with him, listening to him, offering encouragement as I could, trying from a distance to walk with him. At times in our conversation he would be quiet and effusive in gratitude, other moments combative and enraged. I've known that place of emotional vacillation well. He told me some of his story, and I shared a bit of mine. Over the coming days, Brandon and I talked a few more times before eventually losing touch. I hoped I'd been a help in some way. Later that week, I wrote a blog post called "If You Stick Around," inspired by Brandon and the seemingly countless people struggling to stay, despite the urge within them not to. Here's part of what I wrote:

> If you stick around, you will reach a spot that the sadness won't let you see right now—you'll reach tomorrow. And that place is filled with possibility. It is a day you've never been to. It is not this terrible day. There, you will not feel exactly what you are feeling right now. You may be stronger or see things differently or find a clearing and life may look a way it hasn't in a long time: it may look worth staying for.

A few weeks ago, I was overjoyed to see Brandon's name in my in-box. He began by reminding me of our conversation that night three years ago. (I hadn't forgotten.) He said he wanted to thank me for the time I spent with him and for the kindness I showed him. He concluded his message by saying, "I just wanted you to know that I stuck around—and I'm so glad that I did." Yes, persisting in our careers and our relationships and in the fight for justice are all vitally important efforts, but staying is also a matter of self-care and even survival. Sometimes the *staying* we do isn't to resurrect our careers or nurture a romantic relationship or start a business or pass legislation: sometimes it's to just keep on living.

It's deflating to watch *anyone* who's made for greatness stop before they get all the way there. Persistence is the time-released fuel for that journey, and it is invaluable in matters of love and work and being. There's a saying intended to help people move on from un-healthy or unproductive relationships, jobs, and endeavors: "When the horse is dead—dismount." That might be the right move, but it might not be. Sometimes you need to stay in the saddle a bit longer. Sometimes the horse is just exhausted and waiting for its second wind. Right now the world needs persistent people. It needs people who will stay. The stayers are often those who are just stubborn enough or driven enough or defiant enough or enough of a pain in the ass to keep going when stopping seems the prudent deci-sion, those with the steadfast insistence on continuing when the act seems counterintuitive. If you stick around long enough, you'll save somebody, I promise you. You might save yourself in the process. You'll likely save the world.

"I BELIEVE THERE'S A HERO IN ALL OF US."

—MAY PARKER

WONDER

When Peter Parker first begins to realize the bodily effects of being bitten by a radioactive spider, he transforms *twice*. First into a gravity-defying high school student capable of sticking to walls, firing ropes of webbing from his wrists, and propelling himself around New York City skyscrapers like they're a set of oversize monkey bars. But also, and simultaneously, he becomes a wide-eyed, exuberant child whose only fitting response to such overwhelming, uncontainable elation is "WOO-HOO!" There, he becomes both Spider-Man *and* the buoyant little boy he once was, embracing his new identity with all the responsibility it carries, while also operating from a place of innocence that allows him to fully and appropriately marvel at it all without the cynicism and

157

sarcasm he usually wields. We watch Peter catapulting himself with abandon across rooftops, and we vicariously revel in the way he sees his city with new eyes, and how explosively joyful that moment is. We're a little jealous, too.

Such unbridled awe is rare for us most of the time. As we get older we are increasingly starved of wonder. Overscheduled and overtired, consumed with our growing to-do lists and our bulging in-boxes and the ever-breaking bad news, we spend our days fighting fires at home, managing crises at work, and contemplating disasters in Washington. So much of our daily energies are marshaled toward trying to beat back negativity and subjugate frustration—it's exhausting. I hear it in the voices of people I meet as I travel the country, I read it in strangers' exchanges on social media, and I see it in my own countenance: the pervasive weariness that leaves little bandwidth for much else. In this state of perpetual soul fatigue, it's easy for us to drift into wonderlessness in two distinctly different but equally hope-destroying ways. First, we're no longer able to notice the staggering beauty hiding in plain sight all around us, in nature and people and food and music. Second, we stop believing in the invisible magic of what we *can't* see, the possibility that there may be something more than our senses can capture. In either case, when the lenses through which we view the world are clouded, we lose the ability to be wonderfully surprised by life—and we can't afford that now.

It's been said that familiarity breeds contempt, but in my experience it more likely tends to breed blindness. It should be easy to be continually amazed by our surroundings: the striking colors of a sunset, the perfect symmetry of seeds on the surface of a strawberry, the feel of an evening breeze pushing back our hair, or the unique song of our child's laughter ringing out from the next room. Awe-inspiring, breath-stealing stuff is rarely out of reach. But more often than not, we simply stop seeing these things with any fitting reverence because we're so used to their presence and because we're too harried and distracted to look carefully anymore. As nature and people and colors and sounds become commonplace, they have a way of gradually becoming invisible: white noise that barely registers in our awareness. If we *do* find ourselves able to be moved by life's simple blessings, it's often when we're traveling or on vacation or just returning home from a long time away. In those moments, outside of our familiar routine, we're more receptive to awe, more intentionally seeking out beauty—we're actively cultivating wonder. Imagine how differently we'd see our daily, seemingly mundane existence if we could do the same in the places and with the people we spend in our ordinary.

It's a Wonderful Life is one of my favorite movies (Christmas or otherwise), because it's essentially about a man going blind and then regaining his sight. George Bailey finds himself overwhelmed by the difficulties of the day and taking his very existence for granted: his wife, his children, his brother, the friends he's made, the town he's spent his life in. He even begins to resent it all and wishes it away. With the help of Clarence, an affable, clumsy angel-in-training, George gets the gift of being able to see it all again with fresh eyes, to notice how *wonder-filled* his seemingly ordinary life actually is, with all its troubles and monotony. He doesn't get a new life; he gets new lenses to accurately view the one he already has. In the final moments of the film we watch him standing in reverent awe of everything—his split lip, the falling snow, the flower petals in his pocket, the rickety hallway banister, the faces of neighbors. Similarly, we can recapture some of this same wide-open appreciation for our *everyday* lives, and we don't need an archangel following us around to do it.

There's a story in the Bible's Old Testament about a shepherd named Moses, who hears God speak through a burning bush. As he happens upon the flaming bit of shrubbery, Moses is understandably curious, and when he steps closer to investigate, God says: "Take off your sandals, for the place where you are standing is holy ground." The spot is likely one Moses has found himself on hundreds of times in his travels as a shepherd. The difference now is Moses' new awareness of it. The ordinary is transformed because Moses can see it clearly in all its glory. God's instruction for him to remove his shoes is the invitation to sense the sacred space his feet are standing upon. You have this invitation every day to notice all that you take for granted, the beauty in your midst that you may have lost sight of. Whether you're religious or not, this story can be a prompt to be mindful of where you are, to have a reverence for the moment, to remember that the place where you are standing is always holy ground, always a sacred space. This is what wonder looks like.

Sometimes wonder is about seeing the physical world around you with new eyes—and other times it's about straining to see even more. You probably have a memory of being at a parade or a concert as a child and having trouble seeing because you were too short. You could make out flashes of light and color between the taller, larger silhouettes; you could hear the swirling sounds of music and applause, and you caught strobe light glimpses of it all, but the crowd partially obscured it. So you steadied yourself against something or someone and you stood on tiptoe in an effort to take in the full glory of it all, to see what you couldn't from your limited vantage point.

This "living on tiptoe" is a way to understand the specific wonder of spirituality, that looking with expectancy to see beyond what we currently can, because we sense there is something extraordinary out there, just past our usual field of vision. Whether you practice an organized religion or a personal spirituality, or you simply entertain the possibility of some greater force at work in the world that you call God or karma or the universe or mojo—at the heart of *any* belief in the mystical is an ability to coexist with unanswered questions, to embrace the elusive mysteries, and to acknowledge that there are things here that *do* defy explanation.

I've been a Christian for most of my life and a pastor for more than two decades, and until now I haven't mentioned God or faith or religion much in these pages. If you're a Christian and were expecting doctrine, this may be causing you some distress (if you haven't already closed the book and departed). But this isn't a book about theology; it's an invitation to be the kind of person the world needs, and you don't need to subscribe to a certain spiritual tradition in order to be such a person. I'm not concerned with your specific religious worldview, but I am interested in *how you see the world*: in what you believe about this journey, the way you experience the intangibles of this life, and the reverence you have for it all—your *practical spirituality*, if you will.

My Christian faith tradition calls the eyes the "window to the soul," which makes perfect sense, because a spirituality of wonder is all about *how we see*, the lenses through which we view our existence and our purpose and other people. Whether we're marveling at miracles, or examining coincidences, or meditating on the unquantifiable yet fully real experience of love, spirituality should make us more thoughtful, more introspective people who want to amplify whatever goodness is at the source of this life. It should yield people whose lives are marked by compassion, truth, kindness, etc.

When we consent to believing in things outside our senses and beyond our understanding, we can find a comfort that transcends our circumstances. At the same time, faith at its best is not a means to escape from this world but to have a greater reverence for it, an appreciation of how magnificent it is, a priority to be a loving presence in it. It also means embracing the possibility that there is information we don't have right now, and that things may not be as hopeless as they seem from where we stand. The pursuit of God, for me, hasn't yielded a sense of separation from the world and the people around me, but a deeper connection to them both, an awareness of the interdependence of everything; the oneness of it all. The older we get, the more difficult it may be to marvel at things like sunsets, and flowers, and leaves dancing in the wind, but we need to. We need to remember that we are inextricably part of a singular masterpiece that began well before we arrived and will continue long after we've gone, so that we understand the imperative to live fully and urgently in the moment.

One of the ways we can refocus our eyes to see with wonder is to embrace everyday rituals and be intentional about noticing how much bigger or more meaningful they are than they appear on the surface. For example, packing a lunch for your middle schooler might be a fully mundane activity, even one that annoys you, until you consider your son or daughter sitting in the cafeteria the next day, surrounded by friends and laughing, being silly, or sitting quietly, feeling deflated. As you choose the items and place them carefully in the bag, think about how they will fuel your child's body and mind, the way a piece of fruit or slice of bread will literally become part of them and sustain them that day. In ways you really can't fully comprehend, you aren't just packing their lunch, you're preparing to be present with them in the future during this meal. This activity may not cause you to find religious faith or suddenly believe in God, but it sure as heck might give you a new reverence for the sacred significance of the act.

Another way you can cultivate wonder is to change your perspective—literally. As a young boy I used to spend hours every week climbing the massive oak tree in our front yard. After a while I'd scale it nimbly from memory, get to the highest point, and nestle down into a cozy web of branches there in the canopy. With a peanut butter and banana sandwich and a comic book, I'd survey the neighborhood, and everything would look different than it did when I was on the ground a few seconds earlier—I could see the day with new eyes. You may have outgrown your capacity to safely scale oak trees, but you can still find ways to get a different point of view, to intentionally pull yourself from the kind of ruts in which we're all prone to get stuck. This may be as simple as driving a new route to work, or rearranging your furniture, or putting away your phone as you walk through campus. These can all make you more aware or differently aware than you might otherwise be. It might change the way you see things you've been looking at the same way for too long.

In overfilled days, speed is a wonder-stealer, forcing us to fly past things that merit our pauses and our reverence. Another one of the ways we can actively counteract this is by simply slowing down, allowing for pauses during days that increasingly leave little space for them. These may be structured times of prayer or meditation, or simply occasions when we shut down our devices and intentionally still and silence and stop ourselves so that we're able to notice our breath or look around or listen closely. These moments needn't yield warm and fuzzy feelings, grand revelations, or anything specifically religious. But the act of slowing down will make us more available in the present moment, less likely to miss the needs of people in our midst, and more reverent in our ordinary.

As we get older, we invariably end up learning more about the world, about how things work and about the way people are. This is a natural and generally really exciting part of growing up. As we acquire knowledge and gain insight, maturity and wisdom come. Sometimes, though, as we learn these things we lose something valuable in the process: innocence, optimism, a childlike faith. Like a disillusioned Dorothy from *The Wizard of Oz*, we "peek behind the curtain" of the image of the world that we started off with. That's often when cynicism tends to creep in and wonder dries up. Like most teenagers, I started to lose some of my childhood magic when I stopped believing in Santa Claus—and then I met him.

As I mentioned, my dad owned a shoe store in the quaint downtown of our small suburb just outside of Syracuse, and I used to spend lots of afternoons pinballing my way around town, rummaging through record racks, eating my weight in pizza, and watching my dad work the room with a smile and a shoehorn. Looking back it seemed to almost always be winter, though I'm certain we *did* have a couple of weeks without snow if memory serves me. One December Saturday afternoon, I started to hear rumblings that Santa was indeed coming to town, and in fact, was only a few doors away from us. He made his list, checked it a couple of times, and was on his way to spread some early yuletide gaiety. The store filled with young families who began to crackle with the giddy anticipation such appearances inspire in children and their gladly complicit parents. Not me, though. I was having none of such folly. I was so over Santa, and in fact quite insulted by the whole charade. As Saint Nick's stand-in got closer to the store, a noise began to rise, and as he walked through the door I slowly backed toward the doorway to the stockroom. Noticing my not-so-subtle retreat, my father turned and smiled, bellowing, "Stay and see Santa!" I felt my anger rise and my face grow hot. "This is so stupid!" I thought to myself. "What a joke!" I pivoted and ran into the stockroom and proceeded to jump into a large box, pulled the flaps over myself, and lay there in the darkness like a magician's assistant waiting to be run through with swords. Suddenly I heard quiet footsteps on the weathered hardwood floors that got louder and closer, until the cardboard flaps covering me were pulled back and the fluorescent light came streaking through—and there he was, leaning over me in the box: Santa. "Shit!" I thought to myself, but I couldn't move or speak, paralyzed with embarrassment. Then, without hesitating he smiled and said softly, "I know you don't believe in Santa and that's okay.

You don't have to believe in Santa. You can just believe that you have parents who adore you and want you to feel loved and want to give you wonderful things. That's a good enough thing to believe in, isn't it?" He smiled again and left, just like that: Santa with the freakin' mic drop to the teenager hiding in a cardboard box in a shoe store stockroom. I know he was just a guy in a suit, but I've never looked at Christmas or my parents the same way since, and I never roll my eyes when Santa shows up, because I've embraced the wonder and magic of what love does when we give and receive it.

One of the ways to become the kind of wonder-filled people the world needs is to embrace *belief* again. This doesn't have to mean that we find or recover spirituality or pursue religious practices (though it certainly could involve that), but it does mean intentionally regressing to that place where we find faith in *something bigger* again, whether it's the existence of God or the splendor of the planet or the goodness of people or whatever potent combination of faith, mojo, destiny, karma, or positivity that sprinkles a little pixie dust around and makes us excited to be part of what's unfolding. People gifted with wonder tend to be easy to spot. They have a joy that seems to require no data and is not diminished by seeming evidence to the contrary. They "look up" when that decision seems counterintuitive. They are solution-seekers, bright side–finders, dream-stokers, and defiant dancers. The world never has enough of such people.

Wonder can save the world because it is fuel for our best selves. It can be powerful medicine for weary souls sapped of hope and can sustain us when adversity comes. It keeps the embers of our younger hearts burning as we get older and face disappointment and discouragement. Wonder is antivenom when toxic negativity seeps in. It is what we steady ourselves on while standing on the tips of our toes, in order to try to see the obscured beauty passing by. So no, you don't need to believe in God or Santa to be a person who sees the wonder around you. You just need to remember how to keep your eyes open, how to stand on tiptoe and—how to keep looking for the parade.

FIFTEEN

"I CAN SAVE TODAY. YOU CAN SAVE THE WORLD."

—STEVE TREVOR

GRATITUDE

Some days I think I'm gratitude-impaired. I'm embarrassed to say that I don't usually do *thankful* very well. It isn't that somewhere deep within me I don't truly appreciate the abundance in my life; I like to think I do. It's not that I don't treasure a family who loves me, a fairly intact body that still responds pretty well after nearly a half century, or a career doing something meaningful that gives me great joy. It's just that I'm often so busy being outraged by the failing state of the planet that I get preoccupied with, well, being outraged. In the course of an ordinary day I find myself frequently distracted by the fight for what *should be*, and I forget to be grateful for what already *is*—and it's a problem.

You may have noticed this same appreciation-deficiency in

yourself lately. It is a common affliction for wannabe heroes in tumultuous times. We ordinary activists are by nature change agents, always looking ahead and pushing hard toward the progress to be made. We are adept problem *solvers*, which means we're also keenly aware of the problems themselves to begin with. In the face of so much discouraging news to weed through, we easily default to unrest, because resting feels to us like surrender to the status quo; our inaction, like capitulation to the malevolent forces.

In some fundamental way, all aspiring superheroes want to create a different reality (which is a good and quite beautiful thing), but as a result they tend to fail to appreciate reality as it is currently configured. Prone to exasperation, frustration, and anger, it's a challenge to be able to look at life in the moment and simply say thank you for the breadth of its blessings.

However, that's exactly what we have to do. For hope to thrive, we first need to cultivate gratitude, because it is the rich soil where the seeds of hope can grow. Gratitude is a prerequisite for the kind of people we want to be and the kind of work we want to do in the world. When things get as jacked up as they are right now, the most difficult place to be—and to be grateful—is the intersection of Here and Now, but we need to find gratitude in the second we're standing in because it leads us to the next step. If hope is the blockbuster movie, then gratitude is the prequel.

Hope, after all, is by its very nature aspirational; it is a propellant forward, toward a time and a place where life, work, health, family, or our world are better than in this moment, where some of the wrong is made right. Hope exists somewhere in the future, a soon-to-be, a yet-to-come, which means it's always just a little out of reach, just beyond the horizon. Gratitude, however, we can hold in this moment; it is present-focused, a sense of what is good right now. It is found in seeing the praiseworthy surrounding us. This might be a good time to do that, to appreciate the view outside your window, an amazing meal you had today, the familiar face of someone you love, the sounds of the birds above you, or simply the rise and fall of your chest, reminding you that you're alive. That in itself is cause for giving thanks: to be here and able to be part of history being made one second at a time.

For our caped heroes, every urge they have to help and fix and fight comes from a deep appreciation of life and humanity. Whether it's the Avengers assembling to save half the population of the planet from annihilation, Batman streaking from the Batcave toward Gotham to take on the Joker, or Wonder Woman leaving the safety of her hidden homeland to enter a world war— the impetus is the same: saving people now and defending what is. Yes, it's about securing the future, but it's also about fighting for the present. This is true for you and me; gratitude is the fuel for our resistance. Grateful people are the boldest activists and the most selfless advocates because they are fierce lovers of this life. All movements of justice, equality, and diversity require thankful hearts that see something worth preserving or someone worth defending. As we do the work of changing the world, gratitude is the way we properly value what we already have in order to cherish and protect it, even as we aspire to more and better. It also reminds us that even the smallest wonders can never be taken for granted.

This past Thanksgiving, as Aimee Copeland's family was going around the table sharing one thing they were thankful for, she gave what would be for many an unusual reply: her right knee. (She's also recently talked about deep affection for elbows, the way they allow us to bring food to our mouths and perform all sorts of other amazing feats.) Such seemingly insignificant body parts might not merit a great deal of gratitude or even attention from you, but Aimee doesn't miss the small things anymore. Every blessing is a big one.

On May 1, 2012, after falling from a homemade zip line in Georgia, her body was invaded by necrotizing fasciitis, a flesh-eating, bacterial infection, which shut down her vital organs and eventually claimed both of her hands, right foot, and entire left leg. Aimee recalls the moment in the hospital while still in a thick, drug-induced haze, seeing her father holding up her severely damaged hands in front of her, asking for her consent to have the doctors amputate them in order to keep her alive. For her, in that moment, the choice was easy: "I knew I wanted to live." She goes on to explain, "I wanted to live so badly I would have let them take everything. I would have been happy just being a head in a jar!" During those first excruciating days in the hospital, Aimee remembered a quote by Holocaust survivor Viktor Frankl that helped clarify this pivot point in her journey: "Everything can be taken from a man but one thing: the last of the human freedoms—to choose one's attitude in any given set of circumstances, to choose one's own way." In that moment of unthinkable adversity, Aimee chose her own way, and it has been a road paved with a sense of awe, appreciation, and connectedness to the world.

Aimee tells me that before her accident, like most people, she often operated from what she calls a "not *blank* enough" mind-set:

the feeling that she was not smart enough, not pretty enough, not successful enough. She was perpetually frustrated. The gratitude came when she began realizing that at any given moment, even with these new monumental challenges and obstacles, she actually always has more than enough. Her sense of abundance now yields a heart that is continually thankful—and not just for the pleasant things. Aimee dispels the rumor that doubts and anger and self-pity never visit, or that she doesn't have those dark-night-of-the-soul, "why me" moments? She does. She simply sees *them* as reasons to be grateful, too. "There is beauty in the raw tenderness of a broken heart," she says. "The anger and the sadness are part of being human." She accepts pain and grief as inextricable from her appreciation for this life; heartbreak and joy are tethered together.

When I ask Aimee how she is different today than she was on that May morning six years ago, she finds it difficult to quantify. "It was a complete paradigm shift in how I see the world," she says. "Before I saw life in one square inch. Now I see into the wider periphery; I notice how much bigger my perspective is." With that more panoramic lens, Aimee's view has been both enlarged and sharpened so as to see the small, easily overlooked things, too. She's found a way of dwelling on the countless blessings that simply allow for our existence and that are so easy to miss: the sun shining, the rain falling, the breath in our lungs, our ability to move.

When I ask her to define *gratitude*, Aimee tells me that she sees it as "focusing on what you have, not on what you don't have." This is both elemental and revelatory, because our inability to be grateful often comes from our perceived deficits: what we *don't* have, what we *haven't* achieved, what we *can't* do. When you've survived doctors giving you a one percent chance to live, and the loss of your appendages, you tend not to do that. You tend to see the victories and catalog the achievements and celebrate the milestones. The glass is no longer half full—it's overflowing.

And since her accident, Aimee has made her life's work about helping other people find the same gratitude in times of struggle. In the midst of her long physical and emotional personal recovery, she began turning outward. She received her master's in social work and launched the Aimee Copeland Foundation, a community dedicated to "helping people of all abilities to find their purpose." Aimee has uniquely synthesized her desire to bring others emotional healing, her love for the outdoors, and her relatively new insight into living with disabilities and created something that is helping countless people, something that would have never existed if not for her personal tragedy. In a very tangible way, Aimee has transformed her pain into purpose. Out of incredible loss, she's mined the priceless gifts that she'd once taken for granted, so that she can help other people do the same. Aimee has overcome insurmountable odds to be here, but she realizes that she's not here just for herself; she's here for people who need someone to show them their inherent goodness and their untapped capacity to persevere—and to remind them to be grateful.

Being an ordinary hero is ultimately about availability. We need to be fully present to truly see people, to be aware of their pressing need and correctly positioned to respond to it. And these three critical elements—people, their need, and our response—are so very easy to miss given the multitude of distractions that threaten to steal our attention away. Most of us perpetually underappreciate the present moment, pulled away by discontent, preoccupied with past regrets and future fears. Gratitude helps us be present for our lives already in progress. Our children are growing at blinding speed, our friends are struggling with divorce, our parents are getting older. They deserve our best. Yes, staying informed and engaged in changing the coming world is critical, but there is life happening across the table or sitting on the couch or playing in the backyard—and we can't afford to miss it.

I was really busy last night. As usual, I'd piled far too much on my plate and found myself at the end of another day, hovering over a screen and keyboard, feverishly typing, furrowing my brow, and feeling annoyed at the seemingly insurmountable, important things still unfinished. I was arguing with a few Twitter trolls, worrying about the latest bit of breaking bad news, and feeling my blood pressure rising. My eight-year-old came bounding into the room (which in itself felt like an interruption at first). I answered her succession of rapid-fire questions abruptly without looking up, hoping she'd get the hint that I was preoccupied and stop asking. She didn't. Then she said that she'd set up a light show in her room and asked if I'd have a dance party with her. For a split second I considered declining and excusing myself, telling her how much work I had to do and how tired I was, and promising her we could do it another time. Then it occurred to me that she didn't want to dance another time. She wanted to dance with me *now*. I realized that there are a finite number of times I'll get such an invitation—and I'd never again get *this* one. I knew I'd never be face-to-face with this specific version of my daughter, at this precise age, in this exact moment, offering this once-in-history chance to dance with her. So we danced—boy, did we dance.

There in the rainbow strobe lights of her room we twirled and giggled and spun, each taking turns prompting the other to follow. We banged on drums and tossed stuffed animals and jumped off the bed. I felt my brow unfurrow and my jaw soften and my anxiety subside in the presence of this undeniable joy. I looked into my daughter's eyes as she bounced wildly in front of me, her face beaming. I could see that this was all she wanted in the world right now—to dance with her daddy—and I was grateful that I had stopped the world so that I could be there with her. I was grateful I hadn't gotten fooled into believing there was anything else more pressing, more urgent, or more important than that moment. I was grateful I hadn't missed this chance to dance.

There is a direct connection between our sense of peace in the present and our ability to be grateful. The former can't be reached without the latter. We know this because we experience it physically on an almost cellular level. When stress and anxiety come, our breathing gets shallow and labored, our heart rate rises, and we struggle to get enough oxygen to properly fuel us. (And this is just when opening Twitter.) It isn't until we intentionally slow ourselves that our lungs can expand and contract fully and our breath returns to normal. Maybe that's a good way to think of gratitude as we engage in a world where there is so much to be overwhelmed by, so much that can make us internally turbulent: it is as fundamental as breathing. When we're able to notice and celebrate the beauty and blessings in the present, a new healthy normalcy comes. Like the inhale and exhale of our lungs, the more we practice gratitude, the more it becomes second nature and the more alive we feel. In turn, the more alive we feel, the more we're prepared to live outwardly.

A CNN reporter asked Aimee Copeland if she'd still ride that zip line, knowing what she knows now. Her answer, not surprisingly, is infused with thankfulness. "Knowing the impact that I have and will continue to have, and knowing how this experience has shaped my life for the better, a million and one times, I would go on that zip line again."

Friends, each moment here is a singular gift, so do your best not to waste it. Ride every zip line, pursue every dream, accept every dance party invitation, savor every second. You'll never regret such things. There is nothing more pressing or urgent or important than being present for your life currently in progress. This will make you more available to people who are suffering—not less. So while the work of resisting injustice, of protecting diversity, of demanding equality has never been more necessary or urgent—while we spend ourselves on behalf of these endeavors, we need to make sure that we don't miss life happening right in front of us. In days like this, living well isn't just the best revenge, it's also the greatest resistance. Be grateful today for the sun on your face, the wind through your hair, your knees, and your elbows—even the tears in your eyes and the pain in your body. Give thanks for this complicated, strangely beautiful life.

PART THREE

TRAINING GROUND

Superhero work isn't easy—in fact, it can be messy, stressful, and down-right painful. That's because you can't really be all that heroic without action. It is not theoretical work. At some point you're eventually going to have to leave the comfort of your Batcave and your Fortress of Solitude, and you'll need to enter the fray and get your hands dirty. As you begin to transform your convictions into concrete measures and your burdens into activism, resistance will be there waiting, I can promise you. As earnest and noble as you might be, and as much as you want to be a help to the world (and have the capacity to do so), you're going to encounter people who will disagree with you, misinterpret your motives, and actively oppose you—and this will hurt like hell. Those who reject equality and diversity, those who perpetuate bigotry and fear, those fueled by toxic religion and politics will not always welcome your efforts, and they'll push back passionately. Your calling to be a hope-giver is fraught with the potential for disaster, but it is worth braving those wounds and bruises and doing the world-saving work that only you can do. Learn how to protect yourself and guard your heart as you fight to be super. Consider this your training ground.

and taken to the sky learns that falling is unavoidable; the skinned knees and knotted foreheads are all part of the necessary path required in order to fly. By the time the credits roll, the protagonists all come to realize the eventual good fortune of their previous breakdowns, even if they didn't feel very helpful or redemptive or instructional in that particular moment. Our failures function this way, like the soreness we experience after pushing a muscle past its capacity as it rebuilds itself bigger and stronger. The point of this life isn't to avoid failure (unless you're a masochist of the highest order, and it's an impossible task even then); it's to accept and treasure the growth that suffering invites you to experience.

My friends John and Tracie Loux know what it is to suffer. They have lived in the refining fire of despair in ways most of us never will. They have seven beautiful children, three by birth and four by adoption. On its best days, parenting is an exhausting proposition filled with sacrifice, heartache, and more than a few hidden tears. All parents understand that to raise a child at all is to bear the tantrums, skinned knees, and high school breakups, and John and Tracie are no strangers to such everyday hazards. But they've seen other far more heartbreaking moments, too. Mattie, their youngest child, was born with Down syndrome and lived his first year in the hospital with an endless array of life-threatening medical complications. He had a tracheostomy when he was only four months old and spent much of his life on a ventilator. Despite an unfathomable set of challenges and tremendous physical discomfort, Mattie was, by all accounts, a defiantly jubilant child, his joyful presence contagious. In photos and videos, you can see that although unable to speak, Mattie's face was more fluent in expressing emotion than any arrangement of words ever will be, and the radiance of his smile makes me sorry that I never met him. He was on the planet far too briefly.

When I met John, Tracie, and their children, they were marking the first year since Mattie's passing, just before his fourth birthday. I arranged to Skype with them in their Kansas City living room to share memories of Mattie and to grieve together. They were still living as Grief Zombies—as I've come to refer to those who are in the early days of loss—moving among the world but only tenuously tethered to it by routine and daily obligation. They were functioning on a practical level, but deep sadness and emotional exhaustion were etched into their faces. As each family member began sharing around the room, the grief didn't depart fully, but it was joined by another guest: gratitude. As they rewound through the incredibly taxing year following Mattie's passing, and the relentless obstacle course of his life, there was a sense of what they'd received along the way, how they'd been fortified individually and as a family.

When I recently asked Tracie how Mattie had changed her, she said, "Mattie came knowing all the things that matter in this life and taught these things to me: to love everyone with abandon, to laugh at life even when it's hard, to make funny faces for no reason at all, to be joyful over the little things, to treat the ones I love like the treasures that they are, and to live every day to the fullest. He taught me that I am stronger than I ever knew and braver than I could have ever imagined. He softened me and turned my heart upside down. For every 'broken' part of him, he reached out and healed the broken in me."

Many of the lessons Tracie learned through the turbulence of her past are only now becoming clearer. I imagine that time has allowed her a clarity she didn't always have in those early, harrowing and exhausting moments. This is how it goes when we are driven to our knees: it always feels like a terrifying, pointless free fall as it happens. It's all chaos and waste. It's only later when the tempest stills and the dust clears that time and distance allow us to notice something more. In the moment, however, often all we can see is the unfairness of it all, the dreams that are ending, the people we are losing, the doors that are closing.

I'd just turned forty-five and was five months into a new church job, when my pastor and boss suggested that I take a vacation. This might have been welcome news given how tired I was at the time, except for the fact that he gave me a start date but no end date. I soon realized this holiday, as far as he was concerned, was meant to be permanent. In that *shit, meet fan* moment, part of me was relieved, as I'd known for a while that I wasn't long for that place (and looking back on it, I had in fact been slowly committing acts of self-sabotage in an effort to expedite my exit). It was a tether I needed to break in order to reach the places of greater purpose, and yet that rejection left me temporarily reeling, trying desperately to wash away the pungent stench of guilt, failure, and shame that comes when someone tells you that you're not worth keeping around. Sometimes it isn't about the hit you take but your condition at the time you take it. Sometimes tragedy catches you when you're already winded and ripe for an ass-kicking. I'd lost my father a few months earlier, and this sudden kick to the curb felt like more than my already maxed-out coping skills could bear. Inside my head it was as *worst* as a worst-case scenario could get—one of those sky-is-falling moments. For a few hours I pouted, cried, ate emotionally, and considered curling up into a ball and calling it a day.

Then I remembered that all superheroes fall, the way Bruce Wayne fell, the way good people do every day when failure and heartache visit. I remembered I could still write my own plot twist. In a moment that felt less like a defiant turning point and more like mere survival, I decided to pick up my recently unemployed, dad-grieving butt off the ground and to keep going. I decided that this wasn't a fitting ending, and that maybe there was a third act coming and it would be worth being present for. Like Spider-Man perched on the front of a runaway train speeding toward a disconnected track, his feet dug into the twisting rails beneath him, his arms pulling to their limits trying to stop it from slamming into the city below, I recognized my personal disaster as a similar moment where everything looked beyond hope, when all seemed lost, but where resurrection could still happen. It could be the place where the story dramatically changes, where the point isn't the fire that consumes the hero, but the ashes out of which he rises.

This has been true for every person on the planet, from athletes to social activists to parents of terminally ill toddlers, who didn't stop in the apparent defeat of their second act, who weren't swallowed up by the dire circumstances, who didn't allow disaster to freeze them—but kept going. Right now you may feel profoundly overwhelmed by a relational struggle, or a physical setback, or a battle you're in. Maybe you need to figure out how to do what all heroes eventually have to do: to hold on long enough to see your failure transformed.

Sometimes defeat comes as an easily definable moment, a

distinct, catastrophic event that brings pain: a death, the end of a marriage, a grave diagnosis, an election result—and these are usually the places we rightly give great attention to as we grieve and lament. But other setbacks are subtler, quieter, not quite as obvious but no less destructive. They arrive in the countless ways we face our shortcomings and catalog our adversaries every day without even realizing it. We accrue disappointments, absorb hurtful words, and see the world gradually go sideways. These nebulous, elusive defeats gradually chip away at us, until one day they demand we deal with them.

Not long ago I had yet another in a continuing series of tiny midlife crises. It was in the middle of my kitchen while cutting strawberries. (I suppose it was as good a place as any.) It came out of nowhere and lasted only a few moments, but it was enough of a sucker punch to the gut to temporarily knock the breath from me and send the room spinning. I was there in the middle of an otherwise ordinary day, when suddenly, out of nowhere, I had a terrifying thought: I'm nearing fifty and I don't have any of my shit together—like, none of it. Oh sure, I have a house and a family and a pretty decent career and all that, but these things are just window dressing, a slipcover concealing decades of stains and holes and discoloration hidden underneath. I was freshly reminded that I don't feel I'm much better at this *life* thing than I did twenty-five years ago—and that really ticks me off. When I was younger, I was always looking ahead to a day somewhere off in the distance when I would be a proper, fully formed adult, when my many insecurities wouldn't be such a regular hindrance, when my nagging flaws wouldn't show up so often to gloriously sabotage my day, when I didn't drop the freakin' ball with such stunning consistency. That day was supposed to be this day. That adult was supposed to be me. Back then, I imagined that the *me* I am today would be a whole lot more refined and well-adjusted and mature. And there over that cutting board, I felt a brief moment of pulse-raising, disorienting panic like an existential dirty bomb going off in my psyche: in ways I couldn't even quantify or name—I was failing.

But almost immediately, a question popped into my head in response, like a cool, fresh breeze clearing out the thick, toxic air surrounding me: *What if the shit isn't supposed to be together? What if that isn't even possible?*

I'd honestly never considered that. In my constant, desperate striving to get and keep it all together, I never stopped to ask myself whether this was ever even a reasonable goal. That implicit pressure we all feel to be professionally successful and financially stable, to have rock-hard abs and well-behaved children, to eat healthfully and find inner peace, to have great skin and great sex, and to do community service on the weekend—maybe it's slowly killing us. Maybe it only serves to amplify our missteps and magnify our flaws and set us up to feel as if we're always falling short.

As a young superhero-in-training, I took on those impossible expectations (or had them placed upon me by others) and have lived with a nagging sense that I have been perpetually underperforming ever since. But when I look at the people I admire, those whose journeys I try to emulate, those whose lives have paved a path for me worth following, most of them were and are a fairly chaotic, cluttered, disheveled mess. They all experience disaster and traverse tragedy. In fact, learn enough about anyone you see from a distance (celebrities, professional athletes, political leaders, social media figures, culture influencers) and you'll realize just how riddled everyone is with the scars of their defeats; we're all bruised and battered by our time here.

Maybe *that* is where the sweet spot of living is. Maybe the point of this journey is to revel in it all, to embrace every unfinished, rough-edged, fractured part of us, because that is where our distinct and specific beauty lies. Maybe wisdom and enlightenment and wholeness are a whole lot grittier and a whole lot less grand than we once believed. Maybe success is simply about moving through the middle of the mess, knowing that we can only be where and who we are right now. Truthfully, there is no finishing of ourselves to be done here. The only time we're finished is when the last breath leaves us and our heart ceases beating. Until then, the illusion of perfection might be the greatest barrier to joy. Maybe we should toss it and flush it and be okay with something a little less than perfect from ourselves and other people. Friend, the bad news is that you probably don't have your shit together and you likely never will. The better news is that you're in really good company. And the best news of all is that you don't actually have to have your shit together in the first place.

Superheroes in the comics and the movies have it easy. They have a pretty good idea of how they're doing at any given moment. They're either getting the snot kicked out of them or they aren't. The madman either has the doomsday device or he doesn't. The world is being overrun by a horde of alien sentinels or it isn't. There is a black-and-white way to measure their success, and generally the whole thing gets tied up into a tidy little bundle within ninety minutes or so, pending a sequel. You and I rarely have this. We don't usually get the luxury of such closure or clarity. Whether in matters of career or parenting or activism or personal growth, success can be almost impossible to gauge because we misinterpret and distort the adversity and challenges in front of us. We experience what seems like defeat or rejection or wounding, and we believe that is the whole story. Because we're usually seeing only the present moment, because we're too close to the trenches, and because we've been conditioned to believe good feelings and pleasant experiences are the measurements of success, we risk constantly feeling like we're failing. Most of us, even in times of relative prosperity, feel like we're perpetually trying to keep our ever-shifting shit together in a room full of fans—cleaning up messes, falling on our faces, and doing damage control, all while pretending that our confidence isn't on life support. We're probably wasting far too much daylight trying to be something we're never going to be and don't need to be to begin with.

There's a moment in *The Simpsons* when Homer (prompted by his wife, Marge) offers a hilariously terrible attempt at consoling his children who've just experienced the sting of failure: "Kids, you tried your best and you failed miserably. The lesson is: never try." That platitude actually seems like good advice when we're trying to keep the sky up and it keeps crashing down on our heads—because we're not designed to hold up the sky. That's above our pay grade and beyond our job description. We aren't made of steel or stone, and we aren't indestructible or bulletproof. Our task as spectacularly flawed, prone to failing ordinary superheroes is to get up every day and go about the work of being a source of goodness in this place as best we can in the moment. This is sometimes going to bring less than stellar results. We won't have lives where the shit is perpetually together, devoid of defeats or disasters, and we should stop putting so much energy into such things. Instead, let's make peace with the failure and embrace the painful lessons waiting there.

There's a good chance as you read these words, crisis or failure is either a very recent memory or perhaps a current reality. We don't get to live much of this life clear of such complications for very long. We're never far from a messy, steaming disaster (or in the middle of one). And let's face it, very few of us ever welcome adversity, ever celebrate tragedy, ever warmly greet suffering when it shows up on our doorsteps—but we probably should. We should probably come out and dance joyfully in the shit storm like no one's watching, because we know we are being transformed. Maybe the falling is more like flying. Maybe what sounds like terrible news, in a strange but very real way will eventually be beautiful music. Yes, you may be feeling like you are in the middle of a catastrophic mess—and you might even be right. You may be completely accurate in your assessment that it's a proper shit show. Friend, as you find yourself facedown in the stinking mess, let me gently lift up your head, look you in the eyes, and ask you one simple question: *Why do we fall?*

SEVENTEEN

SUPERHUMANS— ASSEMBLE!

Saving the world can be a lonely business. It can also wear you the hell out. I imagine that's why Batman spends most of his time looking fairly miserable—at least until Robin, Alfred, or Wonder Woman shows up. The Dark Knight suddenly lightens up when company comes. He finds some welcome buoyancy, becomes a little less morose, and rediscovers a bit of his long-dormant softness.

Isolation can be necessary and quite helpful in small doses, when we withdraw from the crowds and the noise to try to discern what really matters to us or to give birth to a dream, but as a permanent condition it usually turns toxic. Without fresh eyes to look beyond the disheartening situations in front of us, we can become emotionally myopic, only able to see the things that trouble and threaten and burden. With this as our field of vision, anxiety usually follows. In the absence of encouraging voices to dispute the defeating stories we tell ourselves or wallow in as we scroll through our Twitter feeds, we can easily veer into hopelessness. Following the 2016 election, many of us have experienced how draining it is to believe we're on an island, convinced we're the only one who feels the way we feel, the only one who seems to be grieving as deeply as we are. When our politics or religious worldview or our general outlook on life makes us feel out of step with the people around us, we're more susceptible to despair. Without someone reminding us from time to time that we're not alone and we're not out of our minds, we can find ourselves quite sure of both facts. This is why isolation makes us vulnerable to depression, and why we all need a like-hearted tribe to take on the world with.

Most superheroes form a team, find a sidekick, or at least confide in a wisecracking best friend who knows their secret and has their back. They help our protagonists carry the weight of their calling, and it makes us feel better about their plight as we watch it unfold on-screen. In *Spider-Man: Homecoming*, high school student Ned learns about his best friend Peter's wall-crawling alter ego and confesses that he's always dreamed of being the "guy in the chair," the steadfast set of eyes looking on from a distance, the one whose bigger perspective and unique skill set can help the hero navigate himself out of otherwise insurmountable circumstances. Ned eventually gets the chance to rise to this destiny and leverage his particular talents in service of his web-shooting pal, becoming a comparatively unspectacular but perfectly capable sidekick.

If you are going to save the world and not self-destruct in the process, you are going to need a Ned (or two or twenty or two thousand of them). You need people with complementary gifts and different strengths who are *for* you, people who stand with you when things go sideways or you grow weary. They might be business partners, coconspirators, cheerleaders, or simply confidants who let you speak unvarnished truth. They may be people who give you a safe space to process the swirling thoughts in your head, or help you build some part of your mission or dream that you aren't able to on your own. You need other people because they exponentially multiply whatever you bring to the table. Lifelong solitary hero work is a really bad idea on-screen or on Technicolor comic panels—and it's a pretty lousy idea in your head, too. Yet far too many of us have been trying to save the world solo, and it's left us beaten up and burned out and pretty fed up. We start becoming heavy, sullen Dark Knights lumbering around in our Batcaves, lonely and isolated.

We currently have an epidemic of disconnection in America, one that was fueled in part by the divisiveness of the 2016 election. People have severed relationships with close friends and family members, cut ties on social media, and avoided holiday gatherings, church services, and social events in order to sidestep land mine conversations with those they've now come to feel estranged from or exasperated with. As I travel the country or correspond with readers, I hear stories of people who've found themselves pulling away from those they loved and respected, due to their stances on immigration or racial inequality or LGBTQ rights or other issues that have become hills worth dying on. As a result, the election hasn't just been a source of division in our nation; it's created lots of lonely people, men and women pushed to the periphery of communities they once called home and felt part of. Post-election, millions of people are living far more alone than they're used to.

At times intentional separation may be a matter of necessary self-care, a critical movement out of harm's way that can't and shouldn't be avoided. Distancing ourselves from situations and from people who do us damage is often a fundamental step to becoming the kind of people the world needs and the kind we need to be. A relationship may have to end, and the resulting space created can become the stage for transformation, giving us the room to grow in ways we couldn't otherwise. Like many people, I've had to put distance between myself and those I once allowed close proximity in order to be fully authentic, to avoid unnecessary blowups, or simply to retain my tenuous hold on sanity when hateful people insist they're "making America great" by marginalizing someone else. The problem for many of us isn't the fact that we have removed toxic people from our lives—it's that we've *only* done this subtraction without commensurate addition. We've successfully edited out unhealthy entities and removed ourselves from destructive relationships that we may have evolved beyond, but we haven't filled these emotional vacancies with anything comparable. We've started operating from a distinct relational deficit.

Every day I hear from people who are decidedly solitary right now, believing that whatever battles they're fighting, they're doing so on their own. When they connect to my blog, they often tell me that they finally feel like they're not alone, like someone else gets them, that in those who gather there they've *found their people*. Like too many of us, they don't feel meaningfully connected to lots of folks geographically right now. Maybe you understand that. Maybe right now you feel as though you are the last of your kind where you are, that no one sees the world quite the way you see it. Maybe you feel like you're isolated on an island in your hometown, your church, or your family. I can assure you that even though compassionate, loving, openhearted people may seem like an endangered species at the moment, we aren't extinct yet! You are *not* alone, resister, I promise you! The world, even at its most troubled, is still filled with men and women who (just like you) wake up every single day wanting to be a helpful presence. There are literally billions of us walking the planet and believing we, too, are an oddity, feeling similarly overwhelmed and outnumbered. Your exasperation is *not* an isolated experience, your present misery is in very good company. You simply need to find those people who share your passions and your burdens and begin world-saving work alongside them.

Virtual community can be a doorway to such tangible team-building, helping you network with thousands of people who share your values, who are doing similar work, who are pissed off about the stuff that pisses you off. One of my greatest joys is traveling around the country and hearing the stories of people who connected through the comments section on my blog or through a Facebook group I'd recommended. They were able to use those virtual locations as bridges to face-to-face relationships. You don't need to find an army of people to build a tribe of affinity; you simply need to locate one person and start there. Every single movement of justice, every transformative organization, every nurturing community began with two or three people who believed that was enough to start. One of the beautiful aspects of social media is the way it shrinks the world and allows us to find human beings who share our hearts—and we need these people.

In these days when the communities we've been a part of (our homes, friendships, churches) have experienced fracture and up- heaval, we also need to approach tribe-building creatively, to look at options we've never considered before. This may mean you look across religious traditions, visiting a local faith community that you know is doing work that resonates with you and being willing to hold your expectations loosely. It might mean attending a gather- ing where you don't know anyone but believe in the cause they're gathering for, using that as a chance to simply be around people who care about something you care about and letting relationships grow organically. I often tell people that marches and rallies and town halls can be transformative for the statement they make or the momentary impact they have—but also because those places allow you to be introduced to flesh-and-blood people living in close proximity to you who give a damn about the same things you do. And once you do, conversation comes easily, friendships blossom, and your team of radical hope-givers starts to assemble.

The well-worn saying "If you want to go fast, go alone, and if you want to go far, go together," isn't just a pleasant-sounding platitude, it's a testimony to the transformative, sustaining nature of community. Yes, you are gifted and original and uniquely glorious. Yes, you have unrivaled levels of asskickery inside you. Yes, you are specifically equipped to be a catalytic force here. You are indeed an unprecedented presence in the history of humanity, as filled with promise and possibility as anyone. Yet your shoulders (as broad and sturdy as they might be) aren't big enough or strong enough to bear the entire weight of the world. Take it from someone who has pulled out his lower back several times trying to be Atlas: you can't sustain solitary heroism. History is filled with the wreckage of broken, burned-out superheroes who didn't think they needed backup and tried to save the planet solo. Don't add to the list.

As we consider the team we save the world with, we also have to remember they may be much closer than we realize. They may be in the next room. We may have been living in a house full of superheroes all along.

Fourteen-year-old Sammy Cammarota is by all accounts a superhuman being. Known by classmates and school administrators as the "mayor" of his Pennsylvania middle school (where he also serves faithfully as a student security officer), Sammy is a funny, energetic eighth grader who enjoys making people laugh and he's really good at it. A gifted athlete, a fierce lover of people, and an openhearted friend who knows no stranger—he is a walking smile machine.

He also shouldn't be here—at least that was the news his parents, Stephen and Liz, received from doctors during Liz's twenty-fifth week of pregnancy. After a battery of tests, including a 3D ultrasound, an MRI, and a fetal EKG, they learned that Sammy had a variety of brain disorders that had drastically reduced the growth of his head and were severely slowing his natural development. These factors placed him in grave danger. Doctors told his shell-shocked parents that he would most likely be stillborn or at best, he'd survive birth but be blind, unable to breathe on his own, and almost surely spend the rest of his life tethered to machines. Those were the two possible outcomes and either of them sounded terribly daunting.

After a time of intense emotional turmoil and wrestling, Stephen and Liz created a plan, one that would not include machines. Sammy would be born where his siblings had been born, delivered by the same obstetrician, and (if doctor's prognoses were to be believed), he would die in his parents' arms rather than in a nursing facility. They shared the news with their two older children (then ages four and seven) to help prepare them for the likelihood that Mom and Dad would not be returning home with a baby brother, and soon found themselves facing the day that they simultaneously looked forward to and dreaded. Due to complications during a previous C-section, doctors were extremely concerned that Liz could bleed out during birth, and they wanted her to be fully sedated. Fearing she wouldn't be awake to see Sammy for the brief moments he was expected to live, she and Stephen resisted this—only consenting with the understanding that doctors would bring Liz out of sedation as quickly as possible the second Sam was delivered.

Stephen describes that moment with characteristically irreverent humor: "They did the C-section and almost immediately handed Sammy to me, at which point he peed on me. I should have known then what a pain in the ass he would become." It was the first inkling that Sammy would be far stronger and far more courageous than anyone (perhaps other than his parents) realized. He spent the next five days in his mother's room, mostly in her arms. He stopped breathing several times, but managed to keep going each time. No machines. Only his mother's arms and a heart that refused to stop beating. Turns out he would get to go home after all. He would get to meet his older brother and sister. Still, upon their departure from the hospital, Steven and Liz weren't given much hope for Sammy's future, receiving hospice care and preemptive expressions of grief from caregivers who seemed certain Sammy wasn't going to survive for more than a few days or weeks. Sammy apparently didn't get the memo. He was going to write his own story.

Fourteen years after Sammy's parents got such a devastating diagnosis, his exuberant, wide-open, contagiously joyful life is a daily reminder that even the longest odds aren't unbeatable, even the most insurmountable obstacles can be overcome. Sammy is largely nonverbal, but his life still speaks eloquently. When I ask Liz to describe her son, she says, "Sammy has taught me to see the world through his eyes: Everybody is the same. Everybody is equal. He discriminates against no one. He has made me take a look at my own prejudices and seek out those different than me." Stephen talks about the way Sammy's presence has changed him, the way he has changed their entire family, how he has helped clarify life for them all, reducing it down to only those things that really matter, which has been a recurring theme in their family story.

A year into Sammy's life, just as they were coming up for air, Stephen and Liz discovered that Sammy's older brother Stephen also had a very different but equally potentially life-shortening disorder called common variable immune deficiency, which prevents his body from producing antibodies, makes him extremely susceptible to illnesses, and increases the likelihood of cancer. He, too, has endured incredible physical challenges and, like his younger brother Sammy, has both found strength in his family while also being the inspiration for *them*. Talking to the Cammarotas, it's clear that each of them is the hero to the other. "We draw strength from each other; we keep each other going," Liz says of her family. This is what we find in all collections of people who do life-changing, revolutionary work together, whether in families, friendships, non-profits, or businesses: community is a life sustainer. It helps us both see and be the hero.

Regardless of how competent or charismatic or high-functioning you might be, it's just about impossible to change the world on your own. After all, if you take a moment and look back on the superpower traits we've talked about, you'll notice that very few of them can exist in a vacuum, and in fact none of them survive very long outside real, messy, costly relationships. They are all predicated on connection. Compassion needs another's story to invest itself in and move toward. Generosity requires a recipient to be extended to. Humor is magnified when it is shared with a like-hearted soul. Our gifts and abilities are, by their nature, meant to be relational.

I am prone to forgetting this myself. I often head to the beach for a few days to write. There's something about the ocean that dismantles the worst of me. Whenever I find my way to that sacred place where the sea meets the shore, everything within me changes. The unnecessary weight of worry and fear and indecision, some-how it all just falls away with each breaking wave. My breath slows back to a pace I'd forgotten was normal, the deep lines on my face start to soften, my tightened jaw slowly relaxes, and I begin to feel a rare quieting of my otherwise racing mind. As a high-functioning but near Olympic-level introvert, I often find myself daydreaming when I'm there about living such a solitary existence full-time. I imagine disappearing and leaving the world behind to find those unspoiled places of silence and solitude, far away from the dizzying noise of the crowds, where I can hear my heart beat again. And yet, when I *do* find those brief moments of glorious seclusion, the initial relief eventually gives way to longing—for people. What feels for a while like welcome white space eventually becomes loneliness. I find myself texting a photo of the sunset to my wife, or wishing I had my kids there to brave the waves with me, or wanting friends to share the moment with. It turns out going solo is okay in small doses, but cultivating hope over the long haul is a collaborative endeavor.

One of my favorite Beatles songs is "Getting Better" from *Sgt. Pepper's Lonely Hearts Club Band*. Initially a Paul McCartney composition, the song is one of typical, lighthearted optimism sonically speaking, with shimmering guitars and fluid bass lines. As the story goes, McCartney was presenting the track to John Lennon and sang him the refrain, "I've got to admit it's getting better, a little better all the time," to which Lennon immediately sang back, "It can't get no worse." The seemingly oxymoronic line crystallizes the Lennon-McCartney magic: Paul's lofty sunniness, tempered by John's earthly, world-weary realism. One without the other would be either saccharine or defeatist. As is, it's balanced perfection and something far better than it would have been without the collaboration.

Community is catalytic for a number of reasons, not least of which is that it fills in the holes we have, placing us alongside people whose gifts, passions, and personalities become our counterpoint. We're able to see ourselves as part of something much greater than our isolated story. You're undoubtedly really good at some things, and perhaps less spectacular elsewhere. Living and working and dreaming in community means you'll find people who shore up the things that are shaky in you. Sometimes the greatest thing about true community is having people close to you who can see the things in you that you can't see, who can nudge you past a place of stuckness, who (depending on what you need in the moment) give you a hug around the neck or a kick in the behind.

My wife is organized, rational, cautious, even-tempered, and cool-headed. In other words, she's nearly the opposite of everything I tend to be: scattered, emotional, impulsive, and prone to hyperbole. I'm pretty sure that these juxtapositions (along with our fierce commitment to each other and to the vows we made, of course) are why our marriage is headed into year twenty with a full head of steam. Every day our partnership illustrates to me the transformative power of collaboration.

Whether we find belonging in the context of houses of faith, in our neighborhoods, in political groups, or in online communities, we are wired for meaningful relationships, and these relationships help us have profound impact on the world. Community shows us that we are specifically shaped to fit into a bigger picture and helps us find the spot we're made for. It confirms our hope that our lives are designed for collaboration. It reminds us that we're not crazy, or that if we are indeed crazy—our crazy is in good company.

Find your people, cultivate your tribe, assemble your team, and save the world together.

EIGHTEEN

HEROES AND VILLAINS

*I*n the opening scenes of *Batman v. Superman: Dawn of Justice*, the Man of Steel has a PR problem. It's the same one befalling the Avengers in *Captain America: Civil War*. Many people who once idolized them as heroes now see them as the enemy. They have, through poor choices, unexpected consequences, misinterpreted motives, and just plain bad luck become the villains in the very eyes of those they've sacrificed so much trying to save. We see the toll this takes on them, how much it hurts even the strongest among them to be seen as something less than admirable. Their fall from grace is excruciating to witness because we know their hearts and so it breaks ours to see people turning on them.

It's one of the less appealing qualities of human nature that we like to put people on pedestals just so we can watch them fall, that our appreciation can be a fickle and fair-weather friend, that with any success or acclaim there will invariably be fierce and often unwarranted backlash. Whether Tom Brady or Taylor Swift or Barack Obama, popularity invites dissenting opinions. This is true for celebrities, politicians, and real-life role models, but it's true for Iron Men, Wonder Women, and Batgirls, too. A fictional super-hero's abrupt *unwelcome* is the time-tested heart of so many pivotal second acts: the opposition always comes when people move on behalf of justice and goodness. In the stories we love to watch and read, one way or another (whether through citizen outcry, govern-ment objection, or archenemy disdain), negativity always shows up to crash the positive party in progress. All heroes, no matter how selfless or charitable or brave, no matter what superlative worthy work they've accomplished, eventually find themselves face-to-face with people who don't think they're all that *super*. As they encounter those who misunderstand their intentions, criticize their methods, or see them as a threat, *they* become the villain. In that instant the tables are turned, and for the first time they bear the title of Bad Guy—and it doesn't feel very good.

Criticism never does, does it? We almost universally crumble when it shows up on our doorsteps or calls us out publicly. No matter how self-assured we believe ourselves to be or how strong we make our exteriors appear, none of us are ever really prepared for the slap in the face of another's dismissal or vitriol. It always stings. It always makes us second-guess the road we're on or the work we're doing or the way we're doing it. That's why comic books and superhero films can be educational (at least my twelve-year-old claims so and

I'm totally fine with it). They help prepare us to endure (and even warmly welcome) pushback when it comes—and my friend, it *always* comes. Watching Spider-Man's reputation trashed on the front page of the *Daily Bugle* or a bronze statue of Superman defaced in the heart of Metropolis is a necessary reminder that being the kind of person the world needs doesn't mean the world will always universally agree that it needs you. In fact, on some days you'll be deemed the villain by the very people you're trying to take a bullet for, those you're most intending to help. Many times the ones you expected to be most boisterously celebrating your passionate activism will be the ones most forcefully pushing back, and it will tear you up.

And that moment of people's resistance against our best intentions and our most noble aspirations is one of the most critical for us would-be superhumans. It's the time we find out who we are and what we're made of. It is the proving ground where we discover whether or not the whys of our efforts are stronger than the sometimes terribly ugly responses they bring our way. When we move toward becoming the best version of ourselves, when we seek to fix what is broken in the world and to make it more humane, we find out if these endeavors are worth the disturbance they cause us and the sacrifices required of us. Our activism, our advocacy, and our giving a damn will invariably put us in harm's way, and we'll experience opposition from those who see our efforts as a threat. Touch people's fears and rattle their place of privilege, and their responses will often be severe.

This book exists precisely for these bedrock-shaking moments when we try to move something from heart to hand, when we attempt to become super*doers* despite the pushback along the way and the obstacles others place in our paths. Without actually being able to step into the tumult and absorb the negative responses to the changes we're hoping to make (and have been talking about), without being able to see if our convictions can bear the weight of the adversity they invite, everything up until this point is theoretical, just an exercise in creative and colorful daydreaming. Our calling is to make the transition from being people who lament, wring their hands, and long for a better world, to those who roll up their sleeves and build it together.

The dream itself (as beautiful as it is) won't actually accomplish anything—only our hands getting dirty and our feet hitting the ground will do that. Being outraged at injustice doesn't do much for the victims of that injustice; taking action does. But that's a hell of a lot harder than outrage alone, which is why most people gladly settle for living vicariously through spandex-clad, muscle-bound, CGI demigods.

Though it shouldn't be, living in a way that cultivates joy and kindness is often a movement upstream, especially in America right now. We are, after all, attempting to fill in the gaps, whether of compassion, generosity, humility, etc. The mere fact that those gaps exist means that as we work we will be agents of transformation, revolutionaries who are adjusting the status quo, much to the chagrin of those who're perfectly fine with it. At the heart of these pages is a call for *change*—and you know how most people respond to that. There will invariably be resistance to any good thing we attempt to do, and often it will come from the places we least expect and the people we most treasure. That's when it really hurts. It's one thing to battle back the darkness and self-doubt and critique that come from *within*, but it's another matter altogether when other people oppose us, many we respect and even love. This is a rubber-meet-road moment for our resolve.

My friend Tara is trying to do the work of a superhero, even while some people—including those closest to her—would cast her as a villain for those efforts. Having lived most of her life as a "blue believer" in the Bible Belt, Tara was used to being the odd person out in family gatherings due to her liberal political views and more left-leaning spirituality. Ironically, the more she became an advocate for equality and justice and the more she spoke out on behalf of marginalized communities, the more her own community seemed to marginalize her. (I like to call her the "white sheep" of her family.) Tara had been used to living in that tension between what she believed and those she loved, but in the past year she watched the schism widen and the expanse grow between her and her family and circle of friends. As she became more outspoken in her politics and more explicit in her activism for progressive causes, Tara grew increasingly certain of her calling and started working for a local political organization. In her advocacy work for the LGBTQ community, in championing racial justice, and in elevating the voices of marginalized communities she found that sweet spot of the world's need and her wiring, and day by day she was discovering the depths and heights of her own superhumanity.

Yet as her interior life was blossoming and her sense of purpose coming to fruition, things around her seemed to be falling apart. The new version of Tara wasn't finding warm welcome at home or at church. As she recounted the recent months to me, her voice quivered. "I don't know where I fit anymore," she said. "I feel like

I've lost my church, my political party, and my family. I feel orphaned." She lamented the number of friends who'd disconnected on social media, those who flipped her off and left loudly, and others who just went silent and faded away. But the defiance in Tara's voice was palpable as she said, "But I'm not going backwards, John. I know what I've seen and who I am now, and I'm not apologizing for it."

I believed her. This is what happens when you find the priceless treasure that is your truest true: you'll never want to relinquish it. You'll fight like hell to keep it. Most fictional superheroes (and flesh-and-blood superhumans) have these bottom-dropping-out moments of soul-searching, of cost-counting, of weighing the price of becoming the most authentic version of themselves, of fighting the despair when it seems unfairly high. If you haven't faced some adversity because you're trying to be the kind of person the world needs—sit tight, that day is coming. You will be met with opposition to a cause you've embraced or a belief you've expressed or a decision you've made. And when that moment comes (that moment that feels like defeat), I'll say the same thing that I said to Tara that December afternoon: Rejoice. This tension is the tax on your convictions. It is the collateral damage of speaking your truth and vehemently giving a damn about other people. Finding your voice and using it loudly is precisely why you are encountering this opposition. Don't lose heart simply because of the hatred you're experiencing or the friction it is bringing, because those things are the price of being the most authentic version of yourself—and they are well worth it.

Yet sometimes, even the heroes lose the plot in the middle of the fight, forgetting their original *why* and thinking they're helping while they're laying waste to the city and leveling bad guys with malice. Even Batman gets it wrong sometimes, encountering moments when he loses his way or succumbs to his demons, times when he is conflicted and not sure anymore whether he's the good guy or the bad guy and neither are we as we watch him. So it's also important to remember that sometimes the criticism will be merited.

Something funny about the villains in comic books: they never know that they're the villains. They may be skulking around dark hallways, wringing their hands and laughing manically while unleashing all manner of horror on humanity, and they'll be largely oblivious. They'll think they're the good guys even as they rain down an army of monsters on a city! Through some toxic cocktail of ego, past trauma, and faulty wiring, they'll have convinced themselves that they're doing something necessary, helpful—even righteous. This should be familiar to all of us. This is how most of us go through life: always assuming we're the heroes, never suspecting we could possibly be the problem.

The work I do brings me into contact with thousands of people each month, and not one of them ever believes he or she is the problem. Miraculously, in two decades as a pastor and activist, I haven't met a single admitted racist, misogynist, homophobe, or anti-Semite, and that's because when we're hateful we almost never realize we're being hateful. We always believe ourselves fully justified in our position. (I like to tell people, "There's a fine line between righteous and self-righteous—and you're it.") One of the greatest challenges we encounter as we oppose people we believe are doing really bad things is remembering that ten times out of ten, they don't think they're doing bad things. Everyone believes they have Right on their side, so we need to be gentle with others and cautious with ourselves. We also need to strive not to respond to inhumanity with something less than human, to take on the monsters out there without becoming something monstrous.

On days when there is a great deal to be angry about and all sorts of injustices to be outraged by, we need to be careful not to be consumed by the anger, not drawn in simply by the fight. When we do find ourselves similarly torn and our motives are muddied and we end up living angry, we need the pushback of good people, even though it will still sting.

I imagine you consider yourself one of the good people. We all usually do. We all believe our intentions are noble and our cause just. In our relationships and career paths and activism work, most of us genuinely want to do the right thing for the right reasons. And while that's a really admirable spot to begin, we can't assume that simply because our motives are pure that our execution will be flawless. Sometimes we'll slip up because of that very human part of us that is so prone to fall. We will be vulnerable to pride and self-centeredness and anger, and from time to time those things will derail the work we're doing or damage our relationships or compromise our message. That's why having good people around us to tell us the truth, and having the humility to really listen to them, is so important. Both the heroes and the villains will face pushback. One of the greatest and most persistent challenges we face is not assuming we're always the former.

This is why daily cultivating the ordinary superpowers is paramount to being brokers of hope in the world. Continually practicing

compassion and generosity and kindness helps us stay oriented toward the true north of our pure convictions when pride and ego
and fatigue threaten to move us off course. These qualities keep us
from becoming as angry and bitter and spiteful as the people we
oppose. They help us be *in* the fight and not defined *by* the fight.

Fight hard to stay super, friends.

NINETEEN

ACTION FIGURES

Monique Boekhout balks at the idea that her story would be worthy of including in this book. "I never thought my name would be printed anywhere other than the local paper!" she said through her still thick Belgian accent, with characteristic self-deprecation. I met Monique and her husband, Bob, in 2008, while taking part in a mission trip to Jubilee Children's Center in Nairobi, Kenya, which the couple had been instrumental in getting built. Not far from one of the biggest slums in the country, the orphanage had become home and school and family for hundreds of local children who literally had no one and nothing else.

Six years earlier, Monique had been searching for a way to make a difference somewhere in the world, and her search (by way of a local pastor) led her to this small rocky plot of land in Nairobi and the thirty-two beautiful, bright-eyed boys and girls she'd initially helped raise money for by running the Chicago marathon the year before. Once there on the ground and able to see the magnitude of the need, Monique knew they couldn't stop at just those thirty-two children.

She and Bob created Kenya Orphanage Project and began building a children's center in Nairobi, and through their child sponsorship program, they've devoted the past fifteen years to housing, educating, and mentoring hundreds of young people in Kenya, most recently building a small vocational school, where high school students who aren't able to move on to college can work a trade for four years. In two decades as a youth pastor, I learned that working with young people, whether in Africa or America or anywhere else, is particularly challenging because you don't necessarily see the whole picture while you're with them. You get a brief space and time in their story, and you try to leave something that sticks, and sometimes in the moment you don't feel you've succeeded. Reflecting on KOP, and more important, every individual child who has been touched by their work, Monique's passion welled to the surface as she declared with great certainty, "With those children, we *have* made a difference, regardless of what happens."

And this is the heart of what it means to be the kind of person the world needs, to be a carrier of hope. It is in understanding the incredible impact we make on those we cross paths with, in realizing that the "world" we try to save doesn't have to make news or trend on social media or affect pop culture. Monique and Bob have revised the personal stories of these young people. They've changed *their* worlds, and because of this, changed the planet, too. Their time, affection, and sacrifice have sent ripples into the rest of humanity through the young men and women they've cared for, moving outward from that small patch of land in Africa and into the world.

I asked Monique why she and Bob decided to do something in Kenya when so many other people had just passed through, and she said with a hearty laugh, "Being crazy!" She went on to share that the things they were attempting to do in Nairobi "didn't make sense to other people," which is perhaps an underrated superpower: mild insanity. There will be times when following the prompts of our hearts and stepping into the world with compassion and actually doing what we feel compelled to do will appear quite mad to those who don't see what we see and aren't burdened the way we're burdened, days when we'll be the first and only ones walking the path, because we know how much those we're walking toward are worth. Monique might think she doesn't merit mention in a book about superheroes. I can guarantee that every single child she's embraced through this work would argue vehemently otherwise. To them, she's an undeniable superhero.

So far the work we've done on this journey together here has been largely an inside job, which, as challenging as that can be, is only half the battle. All the personal attributes we've talked about in these pages, every bit of strength and beauty and goodness we're trying to cultivate internally, will eventually require us to move. I suppose that's why they call superhero dolls *action figures* (aside from the fact that it sounds a whole lot cooler than *superhero dolls*), because superheroes *do* things. They act. They help and rescue and smash and save and fight. Sooner or later, no matter how much work we do internally, it's all rather useless if we don't actually show up and step into other people's personal space and deliver that direct counterpunch of humanity to oppose everything out there that feels so inhumane. Our intentions to be helpful or encouraging, as noble as they are, aren't much help in and of themselves. People who *thought* about protesting the Muslim ban didn't form the visible opposition to it, but those who put on their coats, grabbed their keys, and sped to airports to stand with stranded travelers were a visible, tangible resistance to lawmakers.

Over the past year or so, the term *thoughts and prayers* has come under great public scrutiny, as politicians and ministers so often wield the words on social media in response to shootings and other tragedies, seemingly as a substitute for doing anything else. As a Christian and pastor I have no aversion to prayer, but in the face of injustice and suffering, prayer without behavior change or measurable movement isn't something I'm all that interested in. Whether religious or not, heroic people move from burden to action, from heart to hand; they evolve from simply feeling empathy to tangibly expressing compassion. The people who are the difference makers don't wait for someone else to stand up to corrupt power or oppose unjust legislation or advocate for people who are hurting so that they can join in—they stand up and oppose and advocate regardless of the cost. Heroes, whether on-screen or in your school, your neighborhood, or your community, *do* things that everyone else hopes and prays *somebody* would do. They are the kind of people this hurting, hope-starved world needs.

That's why when all hell breaks loose in Metropolis and the

supervillains are running amok and the city is in distress, the imperiled citizens look to the sky, not praying to see a bird or a plane, but the welcome sight of a blue and red figure streaking toward them like a rocket because they know that is the Man of Steel, whose appearance in their dire situation means that hope has shown up, too. They know that with his arrival, they are no longer alone; the odds have turned in their favor, the bad guys are now outnumbered, and their rescue is imminent. The world is filled with people who talk and complain and post and lament and pray. That's all well and good—it's just the easier part of being super. We can do all those things, but let's also do something else. Let's show up.

Being a hero has always been less about ability than availability, anyway. Batman isn't the strongest or biggest guy in the world; he's just the one who got pissed off enough about Gotham City's corruption and violence to don the cowl and cape and head out into the night. Superman is *super* ultimately because he shows up to thwart Lex Luthor. His staggering abilities don't matter if he stays at home. In the comic book stories we love, it isn't the desperate appeal people make to the hero or the hope that he or she will swoop in and save the day that triggers the turning point, but it's the hero's just-in-the-nick-of-time appearance when all feels most hopeless that twists the plot. This is exactly the place we find ourselves standing in. Whether it's the passionate teenagers demanding sensible gun reform, moms declaring unapologetically that black lives matter, exhausted caregivers marching for affordable health care, or teachers pushing back against budget cuts, a bold, courageous minority that acts, when everyone else is still only *thinking* about acting, is invaluable. These folks are the emotional first responders, defenders of humanity who run toward trouble. In desperate days when there is so much injustice and violence to resist, we need the catalysts, the doers—the ones who move. We need everyday activists to carry hope with them.

Activism. That word scares a lot of people. We've often oversimplified and caricatured it to mean standing on a street with a sign and yelling at another group of people across the street carrying different signs, or lying prostrate on courthouse steps until we're dragged away and arrested. That is indeed part of what activism is, but it's also so much more, so much richer, so much more nuanced. Activism is about using our position, advantages, resources, and circle of influence to elevate the voices of people who may have less of those things. It is identifying the holes in the world and figuring out how we are specifically gifted and positioned to fill them or to help someone else do so. Activism is outwardly manifesting our inner convictions; it is the delivery system of generosity and compassion and courage and creativity. At its most fundamental, activism is simply avoiding inaction—and none of us wants an inactive life or an inactive faith or an inactive heart. The values we have inside us *should* be evident in how we live, in the way we spend our time and money, in how we vote and the work we do—and this is what life as activism means. We each need to find a way of impacting the world that fits who we are, our personality type, and the causes that matter to us. We don't all have to be jerk bloggers or polarizing pastors. (That job is taken.)

For you, the beginning of your personal activism might be navigating family political conversations differently, leaning into difficult dinner or holiday discussions instead of stepping away when they become too uncomfortable, and saying words you believe need to be said. Maybe this time these people will be ready to hear you. When coming upon a friend's social media post that perpetuates a false stereotype about people of color or Muslims, instead of just shaking your head and unfriending them, it may mean publicly telling them why the words and images are problematic. Perhaps not because you can change the mind of the person you're speaking with, but because you might give someone encouragement in the virtual crowd looking on and remind them that they are not alone. The point is to show up and speak clearly, and even if it seems to go horribly wrong, to trust that this act in itself will bear fruit that you may never see.

Your personal activism might involve spending time listening to stories that aren't like your own, educating yourself on the ways other people experience justice, religion, family, and America that may be completely foreign to you. It might be reaching across a political, religious, or cultural divide to make sure you really understand who you perceive to be the *other.* Becoming a progressive pastor speaking out on issues of sexuality, diversity, and justice wasn't some decision I made in a singular moment; it was the gradual evolution of my heart as I spent decades trying to be a listener and learner. It was the by-product of getting better stories. Whose stories aren't you hearing? What groups of people are you intentionally or accidentally insulated from?

Everyday activism might involve reading something longer than a Tweet: really studying complex legislation, complicated social structures, and historical precedent so that you're able to cut through the distracting noise of incendiary headlines and speak into the issues with clarity. In times when ignorance seems to be celebrated as a virtue, make sure you know what you're talking about.

Personal activism is also a matter of simply using your voice and sharing your story. That sounds like a no-brainer, but it's actually incredibly difficult, because most of us diminish our experiences and undervalue our contributions. A few weeks after I was fired I wrote a blog post called "If I Have Gay Children." It was an effort to humanize the issue of gender identity and sexual orientation for people who tended not to. The post went viral, quickly reaching millions of people around the world. The next day, I found myself on CNN; the caption beneath that read "John Pavlovitz, Pastor." It should have also included "Unemployed and Currently Despondent." In that moment, I didn't have a penny behind me, no organization sponsoring me, and no promotional machine propelling me forward. I only had honest words coming from a very personal place—and those words were all I needed. This is one of the foundational truths of this book: you have something that the world needs, and you need to give that something to the world.

And your personal activism might also mean standing in the street with a sign, or lying prostrate on courthouse steps, because that work needs doing, too.

Whatever it ends up looking like, finding your specific activism is critical, not simply because it allows you to become a better version of yourself, but because it enriches the world, because it will help another person in distress, because it obliterates the wasteful barriers between people, and because it bends the arc of the universe just that much more.

I watched something happen over and over in Houston after

Hurricane Harvey arrived, and it brought me to tears every single time: an imperiled human being sat perched atop a nearly submerged car surrounded by rising, rushing water, as a group of strangers began to assemble and lock arms, instantly becoming a chain of humanity, one by one extending itself, until finally reaching the terrified driver and passing the person toward safety.

I don't know any of the people linked together in those waters and I know nothing about them individually, but I'm quite sure a few things are true of *all* of them. It's likely that none of them began the day believing they were capable of heroism, or that they would save another life by the time the sun went down. They probably all left the house feeling as stunningly ordinary as you feel right now. I'm also fairly certain they didn't get together on dry ground first to compare theology or to confirm one another's politics or preferences. They likely didn't discuss who they each voted for, their respective opinions on immigration, their sexual orientation, or what they thought of Hillary's emails or Donald's ties to Russia in order to determine who they were willing to lock arms with, who merited being a link in that salvation chain alongside them, who could be a rescuer. And I'm almost positive they didn't first examine the stranded driver's Facebook page or confirm their citizenship status or get their opinion on guns or ask whether they'd acted recklessly to get into the mess they were in before deciding whether or not they were worth saving. Those who gathered on the edge of the churning water saw another human being in imminent danger and, without having to say a word, decided to do something brave and beautiful and redemptive together because the life on the end of that chain was worth it. The inherent value of the stranger sitting in that filthy, terrifying river was more important than anything they believed or considered about one another that might keep them from moving together.

When we see people clearly in need, obviously in distress, we put aside lazy stereotypes, opposing politics, or exterior differences, and we care for them without pausing to examine whether or not we agree with or even like them. We become the best version of humanity, because we know implicitly how valuable life is and we are propelled toward that life when it is endangered. If only we could realize that people around us are *always* in need, just less visibly so. Many of those we work with and pass on the street, those who sit near us at restaurants and across from us on our Twitter feed, are assailed in this very moment by crippling grief and catastrophic illness, by financial disaster and marital failure, by depression and loneliness and the nagging fears that they can't ever shake. All around us people are close to drowning. They are pressed up hard against their limits. They are struggling to breathe and barely holding on. And this is the point. This is your calling. This is why you're here: to be the kind of people who give a damn and give of themselves and get their hands dirty—and save people. Are you waiting for an invitation? Consider this yours.

TWENTY

YOU ARE THE HOPE

*T*he whole damn world is upside down.

I've said that to myself a few thousand times lately. I've looked around at the rising violence and the expanding fractures and the unapologetic bigotry in our country and the world—and felt profoundly disoriented. I've heard people around me speak with abject hatred, and I've walked away from conversations with people I know and love, feeling spiritually nauseated. I bet you have, too. There's no denying the darkness of the days, but there's also no avoiding the dawn peeking over the horizon. Because with all the sleep I've lost and the grieving I've done and the expletives I've let fly and the worry lines I've acquired and the wine I've consumed, I also give thanks because of what I've seen rising up in response to these terribly stomach-turning, hope-stealing days.

I've seen millions of ordinary people become overnight activists, engaging with the political process in their local communities in ways they never have before. I've witnessed vast multitudes march in the streets of this country and around the world in solidarity and shared outrage. I've seen thousands of people converge in airports to defend distraught refugee families. I've seen churches and moms' groups assemble at pride parades to let LGBTQ people know they are loved and supported. I've watched friends leverage their social media platforms to expose corruption and protest inhumane legislation and pressure elected officials into acting with decency. I've seen Muslim bans fail and health-care repeals be defeated and states defying unjust presidential decrees because good people have raised their voices en masse. I've witnessed our judiciary stand up time and time again to defend our Constitution and our people from those who would disregard both. I've watched loud, defiant caretakers of love and diversity outnumber and chase away Nazis and supremacists attempting to intimidate good people into silence. I've seen teenagers lead the charge against the proliferation of assault weapons. I've met thousands of people in progressive churches and women's groups and civic gatherings and humanist conferences and interfaith services all standing together to say that the enmity coming from the Oval Office does not speak for them, that it is not America, that it is not who we are. I've seen the very best of humanity rise up in the face of the most inhumane behavior. Most of all, I've seen heroes being born before my very eyes.

In my book, *A Bigger Table*, I share the story of being the houseguest of my friend Rod at his gorgeous home in the rolling hills of Santa Rosa, California, and I talk about the wonderful hospitality I experienced there. One terrifying predawn morning this past summer, Rod was awakened by the news that a massive, quickly moving firestorm had engulfed the surrounding area and that he and his family needed to leave immediately. By the time they collected themselves, the fires were already snaking swiftly through his neighborhood, the smoke rising over the treetops. He and his wife had just minutes to grab a few personal things and speed away. Soon after he departed, Rod's entire home was leveled to ash.

He and I spoke on the phone the next day, and as can be imagined, he was still in shock. While relaying the final, frantic moments in his beloved home, he matter-of-factly said, "We saved what we could." There is something so profound about these words. *This* is what superhumans do. This is our beautifully simple job description. As we live, we rub shoulders with desperate people in urgent moments, and we do what we can to be of help. We extend kindness, we offer compassion, and we practice generosity. We show up in the sudden and devastating storms of trauma—and we save what we can. This is what your heroes have done for you, isn't it? If you rewind through your story and note the people who've been the difference makers, they very likely haven't performed extraordinary, newsworthy feats or gained the adoration of the nation, but in simple, unspectacular acts of compassion and kindness, they have saved you.

And that's the naked, unadorned beauty of it all, true believer. You are prepared, experienced, and equipped to rise to the occasion, to do some saving of your own. You don't need further information or education, you don't have to wait for permission, and you also don't have any excuses either.

Does that still feel daunting? Here's my advice: rather than always having your gaze fixed on the horizon and being overwhelmed by all that seems so wrong in the big world stretched out for miles ahead of you, focus on what is within reach. Instead of being preoccupied with the towering figures you watch on the news, turn your head down a bit and see who's right in front of you. Look at the people there, the ones you live with and work next to and study alongside, and see the ways you can be what *that* world needs. Chances are, there are more opportunities than you can count, and the small acts of kindness, compassion, and sacrifice you perform in your daily ordinary life will be perpetuated in ways you could never imagine, multiplied and amplified by those you encourage and influence and lift and inspire. No, friend, you don't actually save the whole world in one fell swoop—you simply start by saving the small portion of it you happen to be standing on at any given moment. The ripples of a revolution start right where you drop a stone into the water:

In the place you call home, the conversations around the dinner table, and the quiet, intimate moments with your children or your spouse or your partner.

In the friendships you've carefully cultivated over time, the ones that have endured and that transcend religion or politics or any manufactured barrier.

In the streets where you spend your days, in the churches and shops and neighborhoods you pass time in and pass by and know from memory.

In the lives of people whose names you know, whose stories you've participated in, whose journeys you've intersected with, in whose presence you feel at home.

In your family, your community, your church, your circle of friends—your adopted tribe.

In the way you choose to spend your resources of time, money, and influence—how you decide what is worth giving yourself away for.

In the work you do you come alongside other like-hearted people as you seek to be the kind of person the world needs.

This week I stood alongside a few hundred strangers in the parking lot of an inner-city church here in Raleigh to honor the seventeen students and teachers killed in a shooting at Marjory Stoneman Douglas High School in Parkland, Florida. Such gatherings seem commonplace these days. We came together to remember those who died, to grieve their passing, and to lament the violence that seems to only be escalating. There was certainly a heaviness befitting the gravity of the moment, but there was a palpable sense of defiant joy in communion, too.

As the memorial service began, seventeen local students came to the microphone, each speaking the name of a fallen teenager or adult and lighting a candle they would then carry to the nearby state capitol ahead of the assembled crowd. As each person's name was read, a dove was released into the evening sky, a visual reminder of every victim's individual beauty. A few moments earlier, a handful of young people had stepped to the platform to speak words of encouragement to those gathered. They were prophetic and powerful, and as each of them spoke I could feel the hairs on the back of my neck involuntarily rising as tears continuously spilled onto my cheeks. One of the young men approached the microphone and said, "I am happy to be here today, not because I want to be here during such a terrible time." He slowly scanned the crowd for a moment and then continued. "I am happy today, because I came here for hope . . . and it is here. It is in you—in every single one of you standing here today. You are the hope I needed, and this is why I'm happy, even today." A roar erupted from every direction of the gathered multitude.

That young man gave words to a vital truth about the incredible power of hope and our ability—our existential mandate—to nourish it. Yes, hope *is* a superpower, maybe the most important one, because of the way it sustains us. It is the pulsing lifeblood for weary hearts in dispiriting days. It is the steadfast belief that somewhere off in the distance, terrible things will get better; everything upside down will be right sided; despite hate's booming voice, love will have the last, loudest word. Hope sees possibility despite a mountain of evidence arguing against it. It launches us into the world, even when that world is filled with ugliness and opposition that we'd prefer not to confront. You and I get to be stewards and protectors of hope when it is most vulnerable; like carriers of a small candle in a storm, we keep hope close to our chests and protect it from the winds and the weather that threaten to snuff it out. We get to make sure that there is light still left to pierce the darkness.

You've been given a priceless gift with this life of yours. You get to wake up every morning and run into your living room and your neighborhood and your school and your city, into *your* Metropolis filled with imperiled, exhausted people all waiting for someone to do something—and *you* get to do something. In ways no one else can, you get to bring hope to people who have forgotten what hope feels like.

At the end of your time here, the world will either be more or less kind, compassionate, generous, funny, creative, and loving because of your presence in it—and you alone get to choose.

Friend, you know who you are, you know the beautiful arsenal at your disposal, you know the need and the stakes and the cost, and deep within, you know *exactly* the kind of people this place needs right now.

All that's left is for you to put this book down and to go and do what superheroes do: give a damn and love well and chase away fear and make the bad guys run, and fight like hell not to waste a single, glorious second of daylight you have left.

Lift your head skyward, hero—and go save the world.

*I*t's impossible to cultivate hope alone. As I've walked this road over the past year, I've been continually reminded of the exponential power of community and of the ways in which the people we live alongside lift us, challenge us, and become part of us.

A small army of superhumans have truly made *Hope* happen:

Boundless gratitude to everyone at Simon & Schuster for being such wonderful advocates of *Hope and Other Superpowers* as a book and as an idea. I appreciate you all for lending your gifts, passions, and expertise to this effort, from the designers and editors, to the production and marketing teams.

Extra special thanks to my editor, Christine Pride, for reaching out to dream with me about making this world more loving and beautiful. You've been an amazing and steadfast cheerleader, taskmaster, animal trainer, truth-teller, and partner throughout this journey.

Thank you to Lashanda Anakwah for working with Christine and me to find the right words and the right home for every one of them.

A truckload of superlatives for my literary agent, Sharon Pelletier, and the entire Dystel, Goderich & Bourret LLC team, for having my back, hearing my heart, and watching my bottom line. It's a joy to work alongside you.

I am surrounded by superheroes in this life who give me hope daily.

To Jen, Noah, and Selah. You are the greatest three humans anyone could dream of sharing this life with. I'm grateful for you in ways that words simply aren't capable of relaying. Thank you for sacrificing so much so that I can do what I do. You are my heart.

To my father, John Pavlovitz. Not a day goes by that I don't think of you and realize how lucky I was to be your son. You're still here, still teaching me how to be super.

To my family, especially my brothers, Brian and Eric, and my sister, Michelle. You shape so much of who I am and what matters to me, and I love you dearly.

To the ordinary heroes who bravely shared their stories with me and with the world for this project: the Cammarota family, Aimee Copeland, John Fugelsang, Rabbi Brian Mayer, Terri Aldridge, the Loux family, Natalie Weaver, Austin King Hurt, Monique Boekhout, Mya Hunter and the SpiritHouse community, Rod Wallace, Sarah Cunningham, and Ryan McCarty. Thank you to those whose names aren't mentioned but whose stories inhabit these pages.

To my Patreon supporters, for the way your limitless generosity allows me to write, speak, care for my family, and not need to donate vital organs. You are true partners in this work.

To North Raleigh Community Church and Unitarian Universalist Peace Fellowship in North Carolina, for providing a place for this nomad to call a spiritual home when he needs one.

To everyone who reads and finds affinity in the writing. It is an inexpressible gift to walk with you, even if geography sometimes separates us. You are my tribe.

To the people who are in the trenches of this life every day, fighting for equality, diversity, love, and justice without acclaim or applause or platforms. None of your efforts are wasted.

To all the damn-givers out there who refuse to stop moving toward the hope. Be greatly encouraged.

JOHN PAVLOVITZ is a pastor and blogger from Wake Forest, North Carolina. His blog, *Stuff That Needs To Be Said*, reaches a diverse worldwide audience. His home church, North Raleigh Community Church, is a growing, nontraditional Christian Community dedicated to radical hospitality, mutual respect, and diversity of doctrine. John is a regular contributor to *Huffington Post*, *Relevant* magazine, *Scary Mommy*, ChurchLeaders.com, and *The Good Men Project*.